Carlo's Simple Wisdom

CARLO'S SIMPLE WISDOM

Words of HOPE from a Young Saint

Carlo Acutis,
Giorgio Maria Carbone

Expanded second edition

Our Sunday Visitor
Huntington, Indiana

Published as *Originali o fotocopie?* © 2024 – Edizioni Studio Domenicano – www.edizionistudiodomenicano.it – Via dell'Osservanza 72, 40136 Bologna, 051 582034.

30 29 28 27 26 25 1 2 3 4 5 6 7 8 9

Our Sunday Visitor Publishing Division
Our Sunday Visitor, Inc., 200 Noll Plaza, Huntington, IN 46750; 1-800-348-2440; www.osv.com

ISBN: 978-1-63966-343-9 (Inventory No. T2979)
eISBN: 978-1-63966-344-6
LCCN: 2025933686

Cover design: Amanda Falk
Cover art: Courtesy Carlo Acutis Center
Interior design: Amanda Falk

PRINTED IN THE UNITED STATES OF AMERICA

Table of Contents

Introduction

Shining like an Easter morning: This is how I personally remember Carlo.

We met at the end of an all-day event. It was late afternoon May 27, 2006, in the village of Oreno in the province of Milan. The event was organized by the Catholic magazine *Il Timone* and the *Fides et Ratio* foundation, with Mass and a conference with Cardinal Joseph Zen Ze-kiun, archbishop of Hong Kong.

Some fellow friars and I had set up a booth featuring the books of publisher Edizioni Studio Domenicano, in particular the works of St. Thomas Aquinas and the *Piccolo Catechismo Eucaristico*. A few dozen yards from our booth Carlo and his parents had assembled a display on Eucharistic miracles, and had explained to hundreds of visitors about the many miracles for which there is solid documentation, miracles that have taken place in various parts of the world from the eighth century until the most recent, in Buenos Aires in 1992 and 1996, which among other things saw Cardinal Jorge Bergoglio in a leading role.[1]

A few days earlier I had received a phone call from Antonia, Carlo's mother. We had arranged for a meeting at the *Il Timone* festival. So, I knew I was going to meet Antonia. I didn't imagine I would also meet her husband, Andrea, and their son, Carlo. Double surprise. Or, rather, triple, because I also didn't know that Carlo was the creator of the exhibit on Eucharistic miracles and the book *Eucharistic Miracles and the Christian Roots of Europe*.[2]

At the end of that afternoon, after a demanding day of talking to hundreds of people, we introduced ourselves. We were all tired, but very happy. Carlo had a smile overflowing with contentment and joy. He was putting the photographic panels back in their cases, treating them like something very precious. His eyes were glistening, almost moved to tears. He told me and the other friars about what he had done that day and above all about his joy at having been able to talk about the active and real presence of Jesus in the Eucharist.

After that day I didn't get another chance to see Carlo. I remember, as if it were yesterday, the sound of Antonia's voice on the phone early the following October, telling me to pray for Carlo because he had been urgently admitted to the hospital in Monza. Just as I recall perfectly the next phone call, in which she told me, serene and stricken at the same time, that Carlo had died. I would never have imagined that fourteen years later Carlo would be recognized as a Blessed. But if I had taken more to heart his smile, shining like an Easter morning, perhaps I would have seen further: I would have recognized on his face the resplendent image of the Lord of glory.

Then something unusual happened that amazed me and got me thinking. Even before canonizing him, Pope Francis presented Carlo as a model for young people, as a young man of "creativity and even genius," and spoke of him in three paragraphs of the apostolic exhortation *Christus Vivit*:

> I remind you of the good news we received as a gift on the morning of the Resurrection: that in all the dark or painful situations that we mentioned, there is a way out. For example, it is true that the digital world can expose you to the risk of self-absorption, isolation and empty pleasure. But don't forget that there are young people even there who show creativity and even genius. That was the case with the Venerable Carlo Acutis.
>
> Carlo was well aware that the whole apparatus of communications, advertising and social networking can be used to lull us, to make us addicted to consumerism and buying the latest thing on the market, obsessed with

> our free time, caught up in negativity. Yet he knew how to use the new communications technology to transmit the Gospel, to communicate values and beauty.
>
> Carlo didn't fall into the trap. He saw that many young people, wanting to be different, really end up being like everyone else, running after whatever the powerful set before them with the mechanisms of consumerism and distraction. In this way they do not bring forth the gifts the Lord has given them; they do not offer the world those unique personal talents that God has given to each of them. As a result, Carlo said, "everyone is born as an original, but many people end up dying as photocopies." Don't let that happen to you![3]

Almost a year and a half later, on October 10, 2020, Pope Francis declared Carlo "Blessed." His beatification received worldwide recognition. And again, to my amazement, I discovered that many of my friends not only knew about Carlo's life and personality, but also turned to him for intercession every day. So, I started reading the many biographies that had been written in the meantime. And the resolution arose in me to give a new voice to Carlo's pithy and brilliant words. In these pages I have collected Carlo's spoken words together with his few writings, those that have come down to us and are known today.

• • •

My procedure was simple. I based my approach on the official public documents, collected by the Congregation for the Causes of Saints in the *Positio super vita, virtutibus et fama sanctitatis*, and especially in the *Summarium Testium*, the section of the *positio* that collects the statements and depositions of fifty-seven witnesses at the hearings for the investigation opened by the archbishop of Milan, Cardinal Angelo Scola, on October 12, 2013, and concluded on November 24, 2016.[4]

The words spoken by Carlo and reported by these witnesses are reproduced verbatim and are easily identifiable because they are accompanied by quotation marks and footnotes containing nothing but a number. This refers to the page number in the *positio.* After presenting the quote, I try to reconstruct — as far as possible — the spatiotemporal context in which the words were spoken, and I propose source texts, which Carlo certainly meditated on — like the holy Scriptures and *The Imitation of Christ* — and avenues of study and meditation, always in the light of divine revelation.

• • •

Finally, it is a duty and a pleasure to thank Antonia Salzano and Andrea Acutis, Carlo's parents, and my fellow friars Roberto Viglino and Davide Pedone for the encouragement and many suggestions they provided me, which enhanced the beauty of this book.

— Giorgio Maria Carbone, O. P.

1
First Steps in the Faith

Carlo was born in London on May 3, 1991, to Andrea Acutis and Antonia Salzano.

Antonia — as she herself writes — "came from an environment, let's not say hostile, but one that in any case had little affinity with religious practice."[1] That is, she belonged to a traditionally Catholic family, but not a practicing one. Antonia received the sacraments of Christian initiation — that is, baptism, first Communion, and confirmation. She probably went to Mass only on those occasions, until the day of her wedding. Despite all this, she cultivated a strong devotion to the Virgin Mary.

Andrea grew up in a more religious environment. He regularly attended Sunday Mass, and as a child, before going to sleep at night, he recited prayers with his mother and sister. He went abroad for university studies, during which time he neglected attendance at Mass and soon found himself not practicing.

Carlo received the first rudiments of the Faith above all from his nanny, Beata, and from some religion lessons in kindergarten. When his parents were the ones who put him to bed at night, Carlo always asked to recite prayers with them — an initiative that his parents would not have taken at the time. "It mattered so much to Carlo, and we were happy to please him":[2]

> Despite this slight initial attention from us, his parents, toward our son's religious formation, Carlo immediately showed himself to be very autonomous in this sense. He went forward on his own path all the same and cultivated this love of his for Jesus. He was very interested

> in delving into the life of Christ through the illustrated Bible books that his grandparents had given him. He often went to church with his Polish nanny to visit Jesus, or to bring Our Lady the little flowers he gathered in the park. The nanny taught him to recite prayers, and the Rosary, too. She also brought him, from Poland, as a gift, some sacred images of Our Lady from famous shrines, which he took special care of. The nanny, Beata, therefore, sowed the foundations of the Catholic faith on fertile ground, so much so that around the age of four or five Carlo also began to ask his mom questions about the faith, asking to be taken to visit Jesus at church.

Let's focus on this taste of little Carlo for the things of God. We find something similar in Saint Dominic, the founder of the Order of Preachers, the Dominicans. His biographers recount that from an early age he did penance and prayed for others.[3] Dominic was certainly brought up by his parents in these acts. But his constancy and firmness in them are a symptom of a "mysterious" divine election. God's choosing of the small, including those small in years, recurs in the life of Blessed Imelda Lambertini, in that of Padre Pio of Pietrelcina, to recall just a few.

God draws to himself every human person, regardless of age. Regardless of the stage of life, extrauterine or intrauterine. This shouldn't surprise us too much, as if it were something extraordinary or exclusive. In biblical revelation this truth is well attested. For example, with gratitude to God, the Psalmist acknowledges:

> For you formed my inward parts;
> you knitted me together in my mother's womb.
> I praise you, for I am wondrously made.
> Wonderful are your works!

You know me right well;
my frame was not hidden from you,
when I was being made in secret,
    intricately wrought in the depths of the earth.
Your eyes beheld my unformed substance;
    in your book were written, every one of them;
the days were formed for me.

(Psalm 139:13–16)

Quite beautiful is the account of the prophet Jeremiah's calling: "The word of the Lord came to me, saying: / 'Before I formed you in the womb I knew you, / and before you were born I consecrated you, / I appointed you a prophet to the nations'" (Jer 1:4–5). Also, in the second Servant Song of the Book of Isaiah, it is said: "The Lord called me from the womb, / from the body of my mother he named my name" (49:1). Of John the Baptist it is said: "He will be filled with the Holy Spirit / even from his mother's womb" (Lk 1:15). And when his mother, Elizabeth, hears the voice of Mary, who has just entered her home, Elizabeth herself recognizes that "the child in my womb leaped for joy" (Lk 1:44). John, still living an intrauterine life, perceives the arrival of Mary and her son, the Word who is already alive in Mary's womb, and therefore also of the Spirit, who is the Spirit of Christ himself.

All these facts show that God always draws us to himself, even when we are just conceived. This relationship between God and each of us is radical; it is the basis of our very existence. And this divine drawing has in us a corresponding ability to respond, or rather to let ourselves be drawn, which is different depending on our age. God creates us and sets us in a relationship of love with him. He inclines us to himself from the moment we are created.

In general, we think that each of us responds to this divine relationship of knowledge and love only from the age at which we are capable of carrying out free and deliberate acts, an age we are not even able to identify with precision. Conventionally, we say that it is at six or seven years of extrauterine age. But the facts recalled above — from Scripture and from the lives of Saint Dominic and Carlo — tell us that even before the age of six we are capable of virtuous acts, we are capable of letting Jesus Christ take hold of us, and of cooperating with the initiative of his grace.

2
We Are All Born as Originals

"We are all born as originals, but many of us die as photocopies."[1] It is Antonia Salzano, Carlo's mother, who remembers this pithy expression of his, and adds: "Carlo had understood well, and many times we had talked about how man always risks going astray, departing from the path Jesus has marked out for each of us." And, she continues, "he had before his eyes many examples of how easy it can be to go astray and spend one's days far from the Lord. He firmly believed that in order not to die as photocopies it was important to frequent the sacraments."

We have already recalled that Pope Francis, in 2019, quoted this expression of Carlo's and cited it to encourage young people not to fall into the "trap" of homogenizing fashions, to guard against the "mechanisms of consumerism and distraction." His appeal is aimed at "bring[ing] forth the gifts the Lord has given," "those unique personal talents that God has given" to everyone.[2]

Being born as originals expresses in a brilliant way the truth that every one of us is: unique, unrepeatable, loved in a singular way by God. Each of us is one of a kind. No one is run-of-the-mill, like a photocopy. Every one of us is generated and loved in an irreplaceable way. Cardinal Carlo Caffarra, to illustrate this truth, often resorted to a very effective example:

> You go and buy a daily newspaper: to do so, you need only say the name. If the vendor gave you the newspaper you requested, and you said, "I want the *Resto del Carlino*, but not this copy, that other one," the vendor would

> have every right to consider you a bit … crazy. Why? Each copy of the newspaper is the same as every other, each being the exact reproduction of the same model, and so each is exchangeable with each: It is a series. Is this the case with each of you? I am sure that you refuse to think so. None of us can be interchanged with another. He is unique, with no serial number. He is one of a kind. Number, quantity does not enter into the world of persons.[3]

Dying as photocopies is the outcome of a life spent chasing after fads. Carlo did not chase after fads; he cultivated many interests, but he had no idol, and he detested frivolous and futile things. His parents recall, "He had no interest in all the things his peers bragged about, like the brand of dad's car, the size of the house."[4] And his mother adds: "I always had to fight with him to buy him clothes, because for him one and a spare was enough. He liked classic wear and did not care to follow the fashions. He told me not to waste the money, and that way we could give more to the poor."[5]

Being born as originals also means that, with existence, everyone receives an original plan to live out "a particular mission in life." Carlo's father remembers that Fr. Ilio Carrai, Carlo's spiritual director for several years,

> helped to instill in my wife and me the conviction that Carlo had a particular mission in life, because he would frequently say, "Carlo is a special child," and to him he would often remark, "You're going to be pope." Father Ilio was certainly not a joker, and he was deeply convinced that the Lord had a special plan for Carlo. I would like to point out that this conviction of his came before Carlo's death: While Carlo was still alive, he told

us and him that the Lord had a special plan for him. He was not the only one, as I wrote in the report, like for example that nun who stopped him and drew attention to him as a special kid. We ourselves were amazed at how there was an air of consideration around Carlo, so that everything seemed to move in a positive direction with him present. After Carlo's death, Father Ilio reiterated his conviction that Carlo was a special kid who had gone straight to heaven, and that they would certainly canonize him. In effect, there was a growing awareness of what Carlo was. I had him beside me every day, and only over time did I understand how much he was loved and respected by the people who met him on a daily basis.[6]

3

God Is Always with Us

"God is always with us and never abandons us."[1] It is Carlo's parents who report this statement. They associate it with the memory of the creation of the exhibit on Eucharistic miracles and with the stirring that Carlo felt over the words of Jesus in Matthew 28:20: "I am with you always, to the close of the age." His parents again add, "This was a great consolation for him, the certainty of God's presence among us."

The truth that Carlo recalled, "God is always with us," is of capital importance, corresponding to the very name of God, the name that God reveals to Moses:

> Then Moses said to God, "If I come to the sons of Israel and say to them, 'The God of your fathers has sent me to you,' and they ask me, 'What is his name?' what shall I say to them?" God said to Moses: "I AM WHO I AM." And he said: "Say this to the sons of Israel: 'I AM has sent me to you.'" God also said to Moses: "Say this to the sons of Israel: 'The Lord, the God of your fathers, the God of Abraham, the God of Isaac, and the God of Jacob, has sent me to you: this is my name for ever; and thus I am to be remembered throughout all generations.'" (Exodus 3:13–15)

Precisely when God entrusts Moses with the mission of setting the people of Israel free, God reveals to him his name, what is called the sacred tetragrammaton, because in Hebrew it is made up of four consonants, YHWH, which can also be transcribed as

Jahve. It is translated in Greek as *Egō eimi*, and in English as *I am who I am*, or more simply as *I am*, or *I am with you*.[2]

We have heard from his parents that Carlo associated his statement that "God is always with us and never abandons us" with the last words that Jesus speaks in the Gospel according to Matthew (28:20): "I am with you always, to the close of the age." Now the fact that Jesus, at the end of his earthly journey, after the Resurrection, should say to his disciples "I am with you" means that he applies the prerogatives of Jahve to himself. Just as in the Old Testament Jahve pledges that he is always with the individual believer, with the one who is sent, or with the whole people of Israel (cf. Gn 26:24; Ex 3:12; Dt 20:1, 4; 31:6; Jos 1:9; Jdg 6:12, 16; Is 41:10; 43:5), so also "here Jesus steps into the place of Jahve and takes on his function with regard to the new people of God."[3]

Jesus pledges his presence, which is not merely being there, but is an active and efficacious presence: it is a presence that brings about salvation, that transforms the disciple and divinizes him. This presence is not only promised but is realized in a permanent and complete way. It is therefore guaranteed in a stable manner. Finally, this presence is not limited to the people of Israel alone, as in the Old Testament, but extended to the multitude, without excluding anyone.

Carlo is holy because he spent his life in the presence of the risen Jesus. He never walked alone. The quality of our lives is determined in part by our friends and by the company we keep. If Jesus is my best friend, then the quality of my life expands without limits, in a way as absolute as God is. Carlo's secret was cultivating the friendship of Christ. By virtue of this relationship of friendship Jesus Christ conforms us to himself and draws to us, and ultimately to himself, all seekers of God. One who is on fire sets others on fire. One who savors a delicacy with gusto makes other mouths water. One who lets himself be drawn by

God draws others in turn. So it was with Carlo. Many people have recognized in him this singular charm, a contagious joy. And he himself approached people with fraternal charity, attentiveness, concern, because Jesus is always with everyone.

Jesus did not come and then go away. He is still coming, always. Indeed, he is always in the act of coming: he is the *Coming One*, as the Book of Revelation says of Jesus: "'I am the Alpha and the Omega,' says the Lord God, who is and who was and who is to come [*ho erchomenos*], the Almighty" (1:8); "Behold, I am coming soon [*kai idou erchomai tachy*]" (22:7).

It is Fr. Guisseppe Barzaghi who points out the need to translate *tachy* not with the humdrum "soon," but, more in keeping with the etymology, with "quickly," and adds:

> He who is coming quickly is such yesterday, today and tomorrow. If someone is coming quickly, the "when?" doesn't matter anymore! And how does one catch hold of someone who is coming quickly? It's obvious: quickly! What is needed is an intuition, a cast of mind in proportion to him, in proportion to his quickness. This is precisely theological faith.[4]

And Jesus is always in the act of coming — not for many, as if he wanted to exclude some — but for the multitude, for all. That all may be converted and saved.

We always run the risk of setting up elitist castes. Carlo broke down every sort of barrier. He sought to give himself to everyone, aware that the plan and the salvific presence of Christ are intended for everyone. This universalistic aspect is taught throughout the New Testament. As a simple example I offer the Letter to the Hebrews, which speaks of a plan of salvation with an efficacy universal in scope: "for every one" (2:9); it is potentially intended for all because Christ the head brings "many sons to glory" (2:10), where "many" (*polloùs huiùs*) should be understood not in an exclusive sense, as "many but not all," but in a global and inclusive sense, as "the innumerable many," or better yet, as "the great host."[5]

4
You Don't See God. But He Sees You

"You don't see God. But he sees you and he knows how much you suffer, and he protects you and will always be by your side to protect you, and will give you signs to let you know that he is there."[1]

Carlo spoke these words to his friend Vanessa, the niece of Rajesh, the servant of the Acutis household. She was four years older than Carlo and was going through a dramatic time, the separation of her parents. On this same occasion Carlo gave Vanessa a Bible so that she could come to know God. Vanessa adds in her testimony, "Carlo spoke of God as if he were the most Beautiful. I remember him telling me that he wanted to be shining and radiant like Jesus, and if we all put Jesus' teachings into practice, we would all be more beautiful and radiant."[2]

Carlo's words are a clear echo of the Prologue of the Gospel according to John: "No one has ever seen God [the Father]; the only-begotten Son, God, who is in the bosom of the Father, he has made him known" (Jn 1:18); of the parable of the Good Samaritan, a metaphor behind which is Jesus, who knows how to get close to each of us (cf. Lk 10:29–37); and of the account of Cleopas and the other disciple, who, heading to Emmaus, unknowingly become travel companions of the risen Jesus, who enlightens them, comforts them, and sets their hearts ablaze with ardor (Lk 24:13–35).

"He will give you signs." There is really no such thing as coincidence, nor is it even the disguise of necessity. But, as Cardinal

Giacomo Biffi said quite effectively, "Coincidence is the disguise God has chosen so as to walk among us while remaining incognito."[3] Even events that we usually call coincidental are actually signs; they refer to something else. And so, as signs, they must be deciphered.

But what is a sign? In general it is a means of communication, a reality perceptible to the senses that leads us to knowledge of another reality, different from the sign itself. Written or spoken words are signs that allow us to communicate ideas. Smoke is a sign of a burning fire. Thunder and lightning are signs of a storm. While God knows every person and every thing in itself, without any mediation, we ordinarily know reality through a process that involves the mediation of signs. Therefore, God reveals himself to us through signs. This manifests God's lowering of himself to us. The signs that God uses in our regard are quite varied: historical-biblical revelation, his commandments, his counsels, the events of life.

Now, for me to discover that a reality is a sign, in addition to having a certain life experience, I must also know the relationship that exists between this reality-sign and the reality to which the sign refers. To go back to an earlier example: I need to know not only what smoke is, but also its relationship with flame and fire. The virtue of faith, the exercise of daily meditation, mental prayer, all help us in various ways to cultivate our intellect so that it may be able to grasp the signs and decipher them.

The lived virtue of faith improves the intellect precisely in this direction. It is like a sort of sixth sense that enables us to grasp the signs and discover their meaning, not necessarily immediately, but perhaps over time and in patient waiting.

The words Carlo left us demonstrate that he experienced this enhancement. And in saying "God will give you signs," he was offering simple consolation to Vanessa, his suffering friend. Carlo understood what Psalm 23 says: "Even though I walk through the valley of the shadow of death, / I fear no evil, / for you are with me; / your rod and your staff / they comfort me" (v. 4). He knew that God will not spare us the valley of the shadow of death — otherwise he would have to take us out of this world — but he accompanies us and sustains us in getting through painful or difficult times. God's "signs" brings us the assurance to face the night. So, Carlo helped Vanessa to focus not on the pain but on what is "beautiful" and comforting.

5

Not I, but God

"Not I, but God."[1] Carlo's mom and dad recall this expression of his. And his mother adds that Carlo often repeated it, and that "he liked it because in Italian it rhymes [*Non io, ma Dio*]."[2]

"Not I, but God" seems to recall the words with which John the Baptist responded to his disciples regarding the identity of Jesus: "He must increase, but I must decrease" (Jn 3:30). And as Jesus addressed St. Catherine of Siena: "You, Catherine, think of me. And I will think right away of you."[3]

These are signs of Carlo's faith in the sovereignty of God, and are a symptom of his humility: man finds his greatness in recognizing God and abandoning himself in him. Carlo did all this with enthusiasm and passion, as Luana Pennino, his maternal grandma, bears witness: "He was a kid who lived for the Lord. He was even passionate in his search for God, and it was not by chance that he had prepared that splendid exhibit on Eucharistic miracles which is famous all over the world."[4]

This passionate love for the Lord made him contagious in whatever environment he found himself.

He was contagious first with his parents and grandmother: "Neither I nor his parents practiced much before Carlo led us to the Faith. It is he who led us to God, to faith, to the joy of knowing that it is beautiful to believe in God."[5] His maternal grandma also states, "I must admit that for almost all of my life, despite having spent ten years in boarding school, I was absolutely not a good Catholic, and thanks to Carlo, who from an early age asked me to go to Mass with him and his mom, I rediscovered the faith that had been lost in me."[6]

As we will get a chance to read, Carlo was contagious with his relatives, his friends, the trusted family servant Rajesh, and the people he had the opportunity to meet. No one was excluded from his contagion.

6

Not Self-Love, but the Glory of God

"Not self-love, but the glory of God."[1] This expression of Carlo's almost seems like a development of the previous one, "Not I, but God."[2] It recalls Psalm 115:1: "Not to us, O LORD, / but to your name give glory, / for the sake of your mercy and your faithfulness!"

And it seems like a concise summary of a maxim from *The Imitation of Christ*: "Glory not in wealth if you have it, nor in friends because they are powerful, but in God who gives all things, and above all desires to give you himself."[3]

Self-love is the disordered love of oneself — that is, not guided and lived for the sake of God and in view of God. It is the love that manifests itself in arrogance, in selfishness, in turning in on oneself, in vanity and vainglory.

The glory of God is the manifestation of God's identity, and therefore the clear declaration of some of his qualities, first among them all the mercy that saves.

Carlo was ambitious, with saintly ambition: He set out to make his earthly existence like a declaration of the presence of God's love.

7
Every Minute that Goes By

"Every minute that goes by is one less minute that we have available to sanctify ourselves."[1]

Carlo spoke these words to a friend of his who confided in him that he was bored in life. Carlo's mom recalls that, with gentleness and humor, "he gave his friend a little lesson on how he should have seen things instead. … Life is such a precious gift that God has given us, and we must appreciate every moment of it."

Carlo's maxim resembles the maxim from *The Imitation of Christ*: "Remember always your end, and how that time lost returns not. Without care and diligence you shall never get virtue."[2]

And it translates and summarizes the model of the holy Fathers:

> Through the day they labored, and in the night they attended to prayer, although when they labored they ceased not from mental prayer.
>
> All their time they spent with profit; every hour seemed short for the service of God.[3]

Carlo desired to be a saint. And he aspired to holiness as a reality — not abstract, but concrete — because he knew that it consists in living with Jesus Christ and in conforming oneself to him, or rather in his own conforming of one to him.

This desire for holiness is not in competition, nor, worse, in conflict with the many interests in beautiful and excellently created realities. On the contrary, our desire for holiness and our being conformed to Jesus Christ, in fact, pass through all of our actions and, therefore, through the good interests that we cultivate.

Carlo had many interests, which ranged from reading to films, from computers to videography. His friend and classmate Federico testifies that Carlo "used his time intelligently. … He cultivated his interests with freedom — for example, he read *Quattro ruote* [an automotive magazine] with interest, but at the same time he read the Bible with even greater interest."[4]

What sanctifies is the presence of Christ in our lives. It is living in communion with Christ. He, being always with us, giving us his own Holy Spirit, elevates and transforms whatever we may do, except sin. Even reading *Quattro ruote*!

8
That God May Make Me Become a Saint

"That God may make me become a saint."[1] At the end of his conversations with his spiritual director Carlo would ask for prayers and present his intention in these words. It is the spiritual director himself, Fr. Ilio Carrai, who recalls this in a statement signed in Bologna on April 17, 2007.

"That God may make me become a saint": This is not a stylized formula. These are not words of convention. Anyone who met Carlo in person knows that he was not affected or ceremonious. He was quite blunt and simple.

They are words that again reveal to us his desire for holiness. This should be shared by all disciples of Jesus. They also reveal the awareness that we become saints first and foremost by virtue of the action that God carries out in us. And never alone, but also by virtue of the cooperation of other people animated by the same desire; this is a way of living the communion of holy things and of the saints that we profess in the Creed.

The desire for holiness might seem like a presumption. But in reality God repeatedly reveals his will with these words: "You shall be holy; for I the Lord your God am holy" (Lv 19:2; cf. also Lv 11:44, 45; 20:7; 1 Pt 1:15, 16).

If I claimed to succeed in this on my own, with my own strength, not only would I be deluded, but certainly presumptuous, proud. But if it is God who asks it of me. But if it is God who gives me himself, the Holy Spirit, and thus enables me to respond to his call, then holiness becomes a duty, an almost physiological requirement. Carlo desires nothing but what God desires for him, and so he asks that others also ask for this: "That God may make me become a saint."

We often form false ideas of holiness. Think of a certain iconography that presents the saint with neck askew, with hands clasped in prayer and with eyes turned upward, or with an afflicted and suffering look, with a dead man's skull on the table. Instead, Carlo lived and now shows us the holiness of the everyday life of a child first and then of a teenager full of interests.

The holiness that Carlo proposes to us is that of a life lived, not outside the real world, not following who knows what iconographic clichés; it matters little whether with small or large acts, but lived in its singular existence; also through simple and ordinary acts, and in any case within the reach of a child first and then of an adolescent. God molded him from within, enabled him with the active presence of his Spirit so that everything he asked of Carlo could find in him a loving response and ready agreement.

9
A Gift So Great

"I will never stop thanking Jesus, never thank him enough for having given us a gift so great by giving us the sacrament of baptism."[1]

Carlo's father and mother report these words. They also recall the context: Carlo was about nine years old. All three were in Milan. They were coming from Sunday Mass at the parish church of Santa Maria Segreta, during which the participants had renewed their baptismal promises. His parents recall:

> On other occasions he told us that there are many people who do not realize what an infinite gift it is to receive baptism, and he felt sorry that many people seemed more interested in external aspects like the party and party favors, the gifts and clothes, than in the sacrament itself. More than once he told us of the need to cultivate and respond to the grace received through baptism, and not squander this gift.[2]

"A gift so great": Given that Carlo belonged to a very well-to-do family, I might think that this would be the latest PlayStation, a drone or a sailboat. And instead: It is baptism. And the one to be thanked is God himself.

Carlo's penetrating faith shines through in the words that Jesus speaks to Nicodemus: "Unless one is born of water and the Spirit, he cannot enter the kingdom of God" (Jn 3:5). To convey the meaning of his baptism, Jesus uses the metaphor of being born, because baptism makes us children of God, ushers us into the relationship of filiation with God the Father. Jesus, the Word incarnate, the Only-begotten, is the Son of divine nature. Each of us, being born of water and the Spirit, is brought into the same relationship that the only-begotten Son has with the Father: in the Son of divine nature we are made children, and so we are in all respects adopted children. We begin to participate in the divine life, to be enlivened and moved by the same Spirit who unites the Father and the Son. And thus we enter into the formation of the mystical Body of Christ — that is, we become the living members of his Church. It is precisely with baptism that our divinization begins. Any other gift depends on this.

So, no other gift bears comparison with baptism and its effect of divinizing us. It is an unforeseen and unmerited gift. Therefore, I will be ever grateful for it.

10
To Send His Only-Begotten Son, Jesus Christ

"The greatest gift that God gave to men was to send his only-begotten Son, Jesus Christ."[1]

Nicola Gori, Carlo's first and most important biographer, reports these words. Their context is not reconstructed.

We can relate these words to the previous ones: "I will never stop thanking Jesus, never thank him enough for having given us a gift so great by giving us the Sacrament of Baptism."[2] The Incarnation of Christ is an event directed to our salvation, which ordinarily begins with baptism, is developed with the other sacraments and with our virtuous life, and is fulfilled in the life of glory.

From the point of view of what is called "salvation history," the summit is precisely the Incarnation of the Word — that is, the day on which the angel announces Mary's mission to her and she says her yes to God: "'Do not be afraid, Mary, for you have found favor with God. And, behold, you will conceive in your womb and bear a son, and you call his name Jesus. Mary said, 'Behold, I am the handmaid of the Lord; let it be done to me according to your word'" (Lk 1:30–31, 38).

But we must also consider that God the Father sends his only-begotten not just with the Incarnation — this is certainly the only visible sending of the Word — but the Father is ever sending his only-begotten to us in an invisible way. In theology it is customary to speak of visible and invisible sendings, or missions.[3] In a visible way, the Father sends and issues forth the Word with the Incarnation and the Spirit with Pentecost, on the occasion of specific historical moments. And he is ever invisibly sending and issuing forth the Word and the Spirit.

God the Father loves the human person always, he wants always to usher him into his communion of love, and he does so by invisibly sending the Word and the Spirit. The ordinary way in which these invisible missions are carried out is the celebration of the sacraments. In fact, we know that when one is baptized it is Christ who baptizes. When one is absolved from sins it is Christ who absolves. When we invoke the Spirit in prayer the Spirit is present in us.

The Second Vatican Council reminds us effectively:

> To accomplish so great a work [salvation], Christ is always present in his Church, especially in her liturgical celebrations. He is present in the sacrifice of the Mass, not only in the person of his minister, "the same now offering, through the ministry of priests, who formerly offered himself on the cross," but especially under the Eucharistic species. By his power he is present in the sacraments, so that when a man baptizes it is really Christ himself who baptizes. He is present in his word, since it is he himself who speaks when the holy Scriptures are read in the Church. He is present, lastly, when the Church prays and sings, for he promised: "Where two or three are gathered together in my name, there am I in the midst of them" (Mt 18:20).[4]

11
That Jesus Christ Be Loved and Known

"It is very important to pray and intercede that Jesus Christ be loved and known by all peoples of the earth."[1]

We also don't know the context of these words. Nicola Gori links them to the importance that Carlo attributed to interreligious dialogue:

> He considered it a privileged moment to make the faith and the teachings of the Gospel known to non-Christians. He watched the television coverage of the interreligious meeting held in Assisi on January 24, 2002, presided over by John Paul II. On that occasion he explained that in these interreligious meetings the pope had certainly been inspired by God, because in this way he was giving everyone the opportunity to know and love Jesus Christ, the only savior of the world, on whom the salvation of all men depends.[2]

"It is very important to pray and intercede that Jesus Christ be loved and known": This is the principle that animated Carlo's apostolate. He carried it out in every way, in keeping with his age and way of life — in his friendships, at school, with his smile, with his earnest greeting, with his almsgiving and acts of assistance on behalf of any person close to him and of any class. It is enough to remember his friendship and cordiality with the doormen of the various buildings on Via Ariosto or Piazza Tommaseo in Milan, many of whom were Buddhists or Hindus.

"That Jesus Christ be loved and known by all peoples" also reveals Carlo's catholic sense: he was aware that Jesus is the only Savior of all, and so he must be proclaimed to everyone, all over the world, on every occasion. The universal destination of the salvation accomplished by Jesus entails the universality of the Christian message. It entails the need for interreligious dialogue, the beauty of fraternal cooperation in the field of human rights, and the testimony of Christian charity.

12
A Life Truly Beautiful

"A life will be truly beautiful only if we come to love God above all things and our neighbor as ourselves, and to do this we need God's help, which is given to us through the sacraments, especially the Eucharist."[1] It is his parents who together recount this memory, without relating the context.

Today the word *love* is misused and twisted in its most beautiful meaning. In the New Testament and in the Christian tradition, the English word *love* translates the Greek noun *agape* and the verb *agapao*. *Agape* and *agapao* are terms used almost exclusively by Christian authors. They indicate God himself: "God is love" (1 Jn 4:8). Also that the disciples are called to live with God and among themselves: "Greater love has no man than this, that a man lay down his life for his friends" (Jn 15:13).[2]

So agape — that is, the love that is charity — is first and foremost God himself. And it is also the action with which God touches us, encounters us, and transforms us. By loving us in Jesus and in the Spirit, he proportions us to himself. And therefore he enables us, in turn, to love him, ourselves, and our neighbor, no longer and not only with our simply human love, but with his strength of divine love. This is another aspect of our divinization. This is also the way in which God expands our will and our desires: He makes us capable and able in willing what he wills, in loving what he loves, in loving whom he loves. According to a measure that is no longer ours, but his, divine:

> The love that is charity is life fulfilled.
> Our success is to live agape.

God's help, of which Carlo speaks of here, is precisely receiving sanctifying grace and the theological virtue of charity, which ordinarily takes place when we participate in or celebrate a sacrament. But it also occurs when we pray, meditate on the Word of God, or perform virtuous acts. We receive God's visit and therefore his grace.

13
Dying to Ourselves Every Day

"The more we manage to die to ourselves every day during the course of our lives, the more possible it will be for us at the end of our lives to be reborn in Jesus."[1]

It is Carlo's mother who recalls these words together with their context. Antonia and Carlo had just attended weekday Mass and listened to the passage of Jn 12:24: "Unless a grain of wheat falls into the earth and dies, it remains alone; but if it dies, it bears much fruit."

Dying to self, like the denial of self, besides not being very fashionable, is also the subject of misunderstandings. To try to understand its meaning it is useful to focus on the parable of the grain of wheat. The parable itself is very short and was inserted, together with the teachings of verses 25–26, within a broader framework, verses 23 and 27–28, in which Jesus proclaims the fulfillment of his hour. So, the parable and the sayings of verses 24–26 are "a splendid commentary on the meaning that the hour of Jesus' death and resurrection will have for all men."[2]

With the parable of the grain of wheat, Jesus is alluding to himself, to his now imminent passion and death. Death is an indispensable condition for having life, for rising again to glory. Thus, dying to oneself — which is always a way in which the disciple conforms to the Master — is never an end in itself, but is to bear much fruit: "If it dies, it produces much fruit" (v. 24).

Any ascetic work, any mortification, in order to be Christian, is never an end in itself. But it is for the sake of a far greater good than that which has been given up. It is functional to growing in love for God or in fraternal charity.

The parable plays on the antithesis between, "it remains alone [just a grain of wheat]" and "it bears much fruit" — that is, the contrast between solitude-sterility and multitude-fertility. In the "much fruit" we can recognize the many saved, the community of believers that is established precisely because of the death and resurrection of Jesus.[3]

Moreover, Xaiver Léon-Dufour points out:

> [This parable] about the grain of wheat is an allusion to the *bread of life* that is Jesus himself (6:33–48), to the bread that is his *flesh for the life of the world* (6:51). Starting from a law of creation, Jesus expresses the mystery through which the new creation is realized, and this mystery also applies to the believer, who, united with Jesus, "will bear much fruit"; this is what the allegory of the vine and the vinedresser will develop (15:1–8), saying that the branch must be pruned and above all remain grafted to the vine.[4]

The parable of the grain of wheat is followed by two maxims that explicitly extend the parable's teaching to the disciple: "He who loves his life loses it, and he who hates his life in this world will keep it for eternal life. If any one serves me, he must follow me; and where I am, there shall my servant be also; if any one serve me, the Father will honor him" (Jn 12:25–26). Here, too, antitheses are proposed — *love* and *hate*, *lose/destroy* and *preserve*. These are radical alternatives typical of the Semitic language "borrowed from the biblical tradition of the covenant (cf. Dt 21:15; Mt 6:24)."[5] The truth is expressed in a paradoxical way so that it can be memorized more easily. It is not an exhortation to masochism or suicide, but to make one's existence, one's self, a gift of love: One's life, one's soul, and one's self are safe when one gives them as a gift.[6]

He who strives with all his might for his own self-realization, excluding the logic of gift, of offering, and of the love that is charity, destroys his life, loses everything. He who instead puts his life at the service of God, and therefore of others (cf. Jn 12:26), finds glory and fullness of life.

These three sayings of Jesus — we have already mentioned this — are inserted in the context of the account of the fulfillment of the hour. And they are almost a commentary on what this hour of Jesus entails.

When the apostles Andrew and Philip report to him the desire of the Greeks, "We wish to see Jesus," Jesus responds, "The hour has come for the Son of man to be glorified" (Jn 12:21, 23).

The three maxims are followed by Jesus' confession of his inner turmoil and an often-forgotten theophany:

> "Now my soul is troubled. And what shall I say? 'Father save me from this hour'? No, for this purpose I have come to this hour. Father, glorify your name." Then a voice came from heaven, "I have glorified it, and I will glorify it again." The crowd standing by heard it and said it had thundered. Others said, "An angel has spoken to him." Jesus answered, "This voice has come for your sake, not for mine. Now is the judgment of this world, now shall the ruler of this world be cast out; and I, when I am lifted up from the earth, will draw men to myself." He said this to show by what death he was to die. (John 12:27–33)

Jesus openly announces that his hour has come, the hour to which the whole account of the tradition of John is oriented. It is the hour of the passion, death, and resurrection, to use our language. It is the hour of the glorification and lifting up from the earth, to use the language of John 12:33.

The hour is twofold in nature: "It causes the crisis and turmoil connected to death" and is at the same time "the moment of the extreme faithfulness of the Son, who entrusts himself to the Father and asks that precisely in this hour he reveal himself and carry out his will: 'Glorify your name.'"[7]

In this hour the Father will glorify the Son of man (cf. Jn 12:23). In the tradition of John there are also other "statements that speak of the 'ascending and descending' of the angels on the Son of man (1:51) and of the 'ascending' of the Son of man to where he was before (6:62)." These mean that God is present precisely in the event of the cross: "Since God is present in this death, it is not a vain and fruitless death, but rather a death that 'bears much fruit.'"[8]

Verses 27–28 present a prayer that Jesus addresses to the Father. It is a sort of echo of many Psalms and finds its parallel in the account of the agony in Gethsemane in Mark 14:35–36. In both cases, Jesus recognizes that fleeing from this hour does not correspond to the will of the Father. "Father, glorify your name" (Jn 12:28): "It can be considered as a Christological version of the petition of the Our Father: 'Hallowed be your name.'"[9] And it can be rendered with these words: Father, manifest your active presence in this which is my hour.

Christ's death on the cross is in view of the Resurrection. So it is with our physical death at the end of our own earthly existence. And so also our mortifications and our denial of ourselves are always part of the birth to new life — that is, to the life of the Spirit of the Risen Christ. This is the objective of every conversion. Saint Paul also speaks of this in terms of sharing in the fullness of Christ (cf. Col 2:10). In Christ "the whole fulness of dwells bodily" (Col 2:9). And through baptism and the consequent new life the disciple participates in the fullness of Christ.

From the previous considerations — which you may have found boring and pedantic compared to Carlo's brilliant conciseness — we also gather that dying in itself has nothing sorrowful or distressing about it. It is rather an act of love and gratitude.[10] Dying to oneself means offering oneself to God, giving oneself over to him. "I appeal to you therefore, brethren, by the mercies of God, to present your bodies as a living sacrifice, holy and acceptable to God, which is your spiritual worship" (Rom 12:1). The expression *spiritual worship* translates from the Greek *loghiken latreian*. This is a somewhat weak translation, because the adjective *loghikos* refers to the Logos. By offering our bodily existence to God, we perform an act of worship that makes us like the Logos, the incarnate Word.

14
Climbing Golgotha

"We often live too frenetically and do all we can to forget that sooner or later we, too, will climb Golgotha. In fact, from birth our earthly destiny is sealed because we are all called to climb Golgotha and to take up our cross."[1] It is his parents who report these words in their joint statement.

No man would want to climb Golgotha. Jesus himself is conflicted, tempted to the end. But he himself knows that it is the only way.[2] Even during his public ministry he urged his disciples to follow him everywhere, whatever the cost: "If any man would come after me, let him deny himself and take up his cross and follow me" (Mt 16:24).

St. Rose of Lima, the first saint of the Americas, a Dominican tertiary and spiritual disciple of St. Catherine of Siena, writes in one of her letters: "Let men take care not to stray and be deceived. This is the only true stairway to paradise, and without the cross they can find no road to climb to heaven."[3]

The cross was and remains an infamous gallows. The incarnate Word climbs up and is fastened to it. He does not eliminate the cross, he does not take away its being an instrument of death that brings infamy, but he elevates it to an instrument of glorification — we have seen this already in our discussion of John 12:23–32 — a ladder to the life of glory. For this reason, the Church sings to the glorious Cross: "Faithful Cross, among all | the one noble tree, | no forest offers such | flower, foliage, seed. | Sweet the wood, sweet the nails | sweet the weight you bear."[4]

15
Conquering Self

"What does it profit a man to conquer in a thousand battles if he is not capable of conquering himself with his own corrupt passions?"[1]

These words are reported in the undated statement issued jointly by Andrea Acutis and Antonia Salzano, reproduced in the *positio.* They recall quite clearly the words of Jesus: "What does it profit a man if he gains the whole and loses or forfeits himself?" (Lk 9:25).

Conquering oneself — that is, one's disordered passions — is a classic theme of spirituality, Christian and non-Christian. Lorenzo Scupoli, in *The Spiritual Combat*, writes: "Take care that your enemies (of whom you are yourself the chief) do not hinder this holy silence."[2] St. Josemaria Escrivá de Balaguer writes, "Your greatest enemy is yourself."[3] Also, *The Imitation of Christ*: "It is a hard matter to leave off that to which we are accustomed, but it is harder to go against our own wills. But if you do not overcome little and easy things, how will you overcome harder things?"[4]

A great theologian of spiritual life still little known, Louis Chardon, writes very effectively: "The way to arrive at perfect virtue is hard and scarcely pleasant. ... Trials have greater glory than sweetness, and the harsh treatment that virtue imposes on those who seek it is the authentic disposition to happiness."[5]

God creates man in order to make him a sharer in his glory, in his bliss. The Cross — troubles, bitterness, suffering, everything that we call a spiritual or physical cross — is a trial that allows us to grow in the virtues, to make a qualitative leap in our lives.

16
Frequenting the Sacraments

"In order not to die as photocopies it is important to frequent the sacraments."[1] It is Carlo's mom who reports these words.

In Carlo's thought the sacraments pull us away from the danger of living and dying as photocopies and give us the ability to live and die as originals.

Why?

We have already discussed that the sacraments are actions of Christ today: Jesus, seated at the right hand of the Father, continues to act in history on our behalf, ordinarily through sacramental actions. The sacraments

> are efficacious because in them Christ himself is at work: it is he who baptizes, he who acts in his sacraments in order to communicate the grace that each sacrament signifies. The Father always hears the prayer of his Son's Church which, in the epiclesis of each sacrament, expresses her faith in the power of the Spirit. As fire transforms into itself everything it touches, so the Holy Spirit transforms into the divine life whatever is subjected to his power.[2]

Also:

> The purpose of the sacraments is to sanctify men, to build up the Body of Christ and, finally, to give worship to God. Because they are signs they also instruct. They not only presuppose faith, but by words and objects they

> also nourish, strengthen, and express it. That is why they are called "sacraments of faith."[3]

Moreover, on those who celebrate and participate in, each sacrament confers sacramental grace:

> The grace of the Holy Spirit, given by Christ. ... The Spirit heals and transforms those who receive him by conforming them to the Son of God. The fruit of the sacramental life is that the Spirit of adoption makes the faithful partakers in the divine nature by uniting them in a living union with the only Son, the Savior.[4]

We have just presented quotes from *Catechism of the Catholic Church*. Carlo knew it well, almost by heart, and managed to express its truths with very effective images.

The Spirit of the Risen Christ acts in the sacraments and divinizes us. This divinization is not a sort of homogenization with Christ, it is not a transformation that standardizes us all. It is an elevation of our good qualities and our charisms, our actions and our virtues to the supernatural life of God. They remain our qualities and actions, and, at the same time being grafted into God, they participate in the divine life through grace. This elevation preserves the uniqueness of our person and is accomplished in an original way, as Saint Augustine recognizes in prayer: "O good almighty, who so care for each of us as if you cared for him alone, and for all as individuals!"[5]

17
Being Pleasing to God

"The Lord would not be happy if I reacted violently."[1] Carlo was a very extroverted and communicative child, but also naturally peaceful and so thoughtful and prudent that he risked seeming a little slow. He never reacted to provocations, not even when some of his classmates or playmates got angry or hit him. His nanny, Beata, would have preferred him to have more grit and to react. But despite Beata's pressure, Carlo replied candidly, "The Lord would not be happy if I reacted violently."

Moses was the meekest man on earth, but he had occasion to become bitter and to sin. We can understand Carlo by thinking of St. Thérèse of the Child Jesus, who, about never committing mortal sin, says of herself: "God, in his prevenient mercy, has preserved my soul from mortal sin."[2] The same mercy of God made Carlo meek and peaceable from an early age.

It is even more interesting to note that the goal that attracted Carlo, since he was three or four years old, was to be pleasing to God.

This desire is first and foremost the one confessed by Jesus himself: "And he who sent me is with me; he has not left me alone, for I always do what is pleasing to him" (Jn 8:29).

It is a recurring appeal in the New Testament: "Try to learn what is pleasing to the Lord" (Eph 5:10; cf. 1 Cor 7:32; 2 Cor 5:9; 1 Thes 2:4; 4:1).

And it is the object of the prayers of the apostle Paul:

> We have not ceased to pray for you, asking that you may be filled with the knowledge of his will in all spiritual

wisdom and understanding, to lead a life worthy of the Lord, fully pleasing to him, bearing fruit in every good work and increasing in the knowledge of God. (Colossians 1:9–10)

18
The Highway to Heaven

"The Eucharist is my highway to heaven."[1] It is Carlo's parents who report these words of his. They consider it "his most precious legacy."

It is a pithy metaphor, a sign of his ability to grasp the substance of our faith and translate it into images within everyone's reach.

The Eucharist is the source and summit of Christian life because, like the union of grace, union with the Eucharist, too, is

> the beginning of eternal bliss. ... Love is eager to contract the union that need not end. He makes himself bread, he makes himself wine. And he says to us, "I am the nourishment of great souls: believe and eat, because you will not change me into you as with the food of your body; it is you who will be changed into me."[2]

The Eucharist transforms us into him whom we receive.

In the process of food assimilation, we who are the superior living being assimilate what we eat — pasta, vegetables, meat, fish, etc. — that is, the food is taken apart, broken down to be partly transformed and taken up by our body. In a similar way, when we approach the Eucharist, Jesus Christ present in it is the superior living being, he is the Lord of the living, and it is he who assimilates us to himself. He makes us his body-fellows, his blood-fellows. Precisely for this reason the Eucharist makes it easy and quick for everyone to reach the goal: paradise.

We can compare Carlo's metaphor of the Eucharistic highway with an image used by J. R. R. Tolkien to illustrate the importance of the Eucharistic bread:

> The *lembas* had a virtue without which they would long ago have lain down to die. It did not satisfy desire, and at times Sam's mind was filled with the memories of food, and the longing for simple bread and meats. And yet this waybread of the Elves had a potency that increased as travelers relied on it alone and did not mingle it with other foods. It fed the will, and it gave strength to endure, and to master sinew and limb beyond the measure of mortal kind.[3]

19
Great Fortune

"Many people don't really understand, through and through, the value of the holy Mass, because if they realized the great fortune we have in having God give himself to us in the consecrated Host they would go to church every day to take part in the Eucharistic celebration and would give up many needless things."[1] It is Carlo's mom who reports these words of his.

The value of the Mass consists in the fact that those who participate in it are made present, or rather contemporaneous, to the mystery of the passion, death, resurrection, and glorification of Jesus.

Through the celebration, made up of actions and words, the Holy Spirit leads the faithful to take part in the efficacy of the Passover of Jesus, to enjoy the benefits and fruits of salvation. The passion, death, resurrection, and glorification of Jesus are historical facts, and, as events that have taken place, they can no longer be repeated. But at the same time, they are also facts and actions that concern Christ: "All that Christ is — all that he did and suffered for all men — participates in the divine eternity, and so transcends all times while being made present in them all."[2]

In this respect they are eternal, they stand forever. Through the liturgy of the Church, through all the sacraments, and especially in the Mass, we are brought before the dead and Risen Christ, to meet him and receive the gift par excellence which is the Holy Spirit.

20
Medicine of the Soul

"The Eucharist is the medicine of the soul par excellence."[1] Andrea Acutis and Antonia Salzano, Carlo's parents, both report these words of his.

Carlo received his first Communion on June 16, 1998. From that day he began to attend Mass every day with the permission of his spiritual director, Father Ilio. He tells us:

> He was convinced, and said, that, thanks to the daily Eucharist, people become sanctified and strengthened quickly and are less at risk of falling into dangerous situations that could jeopardize their eternal salvation. ... He loved the words of St. Ignatius of Antioch, who called the Eucharist the "medicine of immortality."[2]

Beata Sperczynska — Carlo's nanny from the age of three to six — remembers:

> He was sorry not to be able to receive Communion when he saw that I was going to the altar. ... I know that Carlo wanted to receive Communion before the usual age, because he ardently desired it. He wanted to be like the Communion he received: convinced that only if one is truly worthy and pure can one be in communion with Jesus, he wanted to be worthy and pure for Jesus.[3]

His maternal grandma, Luana, also recalls that Carlo "always said that Communion is the most powerful medicine for the soul. In fact, I have always thought that this charisma of his came precisely from his receiving Communion every day."[4]

"Eucharist, medicine for the soul" recalls a passage from a letter that Tolkien wrote to his son Michael, who was seeking consolation:

> The only cure for sagging or fainting faith is Communion. Though always Itself, perfect and complete and inviolate, the Blessed Sacrament does not operate completely and once for all in any of us. Like the act of faith it must be continuous and grow by exercise. Frequency is of the highest effect. Seven times a week is more nourishing than seven times at intervals.[5]

21
Jesus, Go Ahead and Get Comfortable

"Jesus, go ahead and get comfortable, make yourself at home."[1] This was one of Carlo's favorite ejaculatory prayers, which he himself had formulated, as his dad and mom testify.

If put to a rigorous formal exam it reveals some incongruities. But more to the point, it reveals Carlo's substantial faith, his familiarity with Jesus, because those are the words that each of us typically says to a dear relative or a familiar friend.

This expression finds its explanation in an idea that Carlo elaborated concerning the Incarnation, as reported by his parents: "He, who is God, chose a poor stable in Bethlehem, because he had been rejected by everyone. I hope to be able to be ever more welcoming when I receive Jesus-Eucharist."[2]

"Go ahead and get comfortable" is the most natural response to the voice of "the faithful and true witness, the beginning of God's creation" (Rv 3:14) — that is, of Jesus. "Behold, I stand at the door and knock; if any one hears my voice and opens the door, I will come in to him and eat with him, and he with me."

22
Always United with Jesus

"My life plan is to be always united with Jesus."[1] Carlo said this to his mom a few days after receiving his first Communion, in June 1998. He had just turned seven.

Carlo revealed an ability to penetrate to the substance of what we believe.

In the last great prayer that Jesus addresses to the Father, called the priestly prayer, a recurring theme is unity:

> Holy Father, keep [my disciples] in your name, which you have given me, that they may be one, even as we are [with the unity that makes us one].[2] (John 17:11)

And:

> I do not pray for these only, but also for those who will believe in me through their word, that they may all be one; even as you, Father, are in me, and I in you, that they also may be in us, so that the world may believe that you sent me. [And I have given them the glory you gave me, so that they may be one, as we are one]. (John 17:20–22)

Rudolf Schnackenburg suggests reading these verses parallel with John 13:34, as they present the same construction, a linguistic homogeneity, and an affinity of content: unity and brotherly love "belong together like the two sides of the same coin: the prayer for brotherly unity in accordance with the unity that exists between Jesus and the Father corresponds to the commandment of brotherly love in accordance with the love that is realized by Jesus."[3] Unity — for which Jesus prays to the Father and to which he exhorts his disciples — is fulfilled and manifested in mutual love.

Moreover, the unity between Father and Son is not simply the exemplary model of the union between us and Jesus and of the union among the disciples. It is the root cause of any unity and union. In all cases, unity and union have a very close relationship with love. Either because the unity between Father and Son gives rise to the Holy Spirit, which is divine love; or because the unity between Father and Son, through the Holy Spirit, is communicated to the disciples in sanctifying grace and charity; or because the union of the disciple with the Son is an effect of his divine love and is also manifested in prayer, in the worship of God, and in fraternal charity.

Therefore, the disciple authentically expresses his union with Christ when he lives brotherly love with other disciples.[4]

There is no goal higher.

All the Church's initiatives, all the sacraments, all our virtuous acts, our entire lives are oriented toward achieving this union.

Carlo not only understood this but he internalized it and lived it concretely.

23
My Guardian Angels

"My guardian angels on earth."[1] This is how Carlo referred to the hermit nuns of St. Ambrose. He had received first Communion at their monastery in Perego and made it a priority to go visit them regularly. He formed bonds of friendship with them and entrusted himself to their prayers. He was fascinated by the contemplative life.

In Umbria, too, he used to talk with the Poor Clares of Spello and ask them for prayers. One of the nuns had taught him this prayer: "Wounds of Jesus, mouths of love and mercy for us, speak of us to the divine Father and obtain for us an intimate transformation." Carlo began to say this often and recognized that this prayer helped him to stay focused on God at every moment of the day.

The prayer takes up the words of the Prophet Isaiah, "by his [wounds] we were healed" (Is 53:5), and associates them with Christ's mercy and love for us. We find something similar in an admirable sermon of Saint Bernard on the Song of Songs:

> Where can the weak find a place of firm security and peace, except in the wounds of the Savior? Indeed, the more secure is my place there the more he can do to help me. The world rages, the flesh is heavy, and the devil lays his snares; but I do not fall, for my feet are planted on firm rock. I may have sinned gravely. My conscience would be distressed, but it would not be in turmoil, for I would recall the wounds of the Lord: He was wounded for our iniquities (Is 53:5). … As for me, what can I

appropriate that I lack from the heart of the Lord who abounds in mercy? They pierced his hands and feet and opened his side with a spear. Through the openings of these wounds, I may drink honey from the rock and oil from the hardest stone — that is, I may taste and see that the Lord is sweet (cf. Ps 33:9).[2]

24
I'm Coming to Mass, Too

"I'm coming to Mass, too."[1] Elisa, a tutor who went to Carlo's house three times a week to help him with his homework during grade school, says that when his mom was getting ready to leave the house and go to Mass, Carlo, on his own initiative, interrupted the games he was playing and said, "I'm coming to Mass, too."

Love for the Eucharist set Carlo apart even when he was a young child. Sidi Perin, his confirmation sponsor, testifies that when he first met Carlo, who was just five years old, he was already going to daily Mass.[2]

Mattia, Carlo's peer and his friend from the age of seven, recalls:

> He went to Mass every day, and sometimes he went alone, if his mom couldn't. He went by choice and urged us to do so, too. I have never seen such faith in anyone else, let alone another kid. He urged us to go to Mass … and receive Communion, which was "a way of getting closer" to God. A kid like that was light years ahead of us! There was a time when I thought he was going to Mass because his mom wanted it; later I understood and became increasingly convinced that it was his personal choice, something he wanted to do in his freedom and from his heart.[3]

His maternal grandmother, Luana Pennino, recalls that "on trips, as soon as we arrived in a foreign place, he would go online to find a church and Mass times, so as not to miss it. It mattered so much to him."[4]

Those who got close to Carlo caught his love for the Eucharist and dedication to Mass attendance. His grandma again recognizes that "it was Carlo in a certain sense who served to ripen my faith, which before was easygoing: He always wanted to go to Mass, and to set an example for him I had to play the good grandma, so I would go with him. That's how I came back to the Church."[5]

Elisa also reports for us, "He attended Mass with devotion and received Communion with recollection, and it was his example that brought me back to faith and prayer."[6]

And Antonia Salzano's cousin, Debora Zauli, recalls "how sensitive he was to the fact that my family was not very practicing, and so he insisted that we attend Mass and pray. He certainly brought me and my whole family back to Christian faith and practice."[7]

25
Whole Persons, Made in His Image

"Virtues are acquired mainly through an intense sacramental life, and the Eucharist is certainly the culmination of charity, and through this sacrament the Lord makes us into whole persons, made in his image."[1]

It is Rajesh, the servant of the Acutis household beginning in December 1995, who reports these words of Carlo's.

In the same context Rajesh recalls that Carlo quoted from memory some passages from the Bread of Life discourse in John 6:54–56: "He who eats my flesh and drinks my blood has eternal life, and I will raise him up at the last day. For my flesh is food indeed, and my blood is drink indeed. He who eats my flesh and drinks my blood abides in me, and I in him."

He remains in me and I in him: One of the effects of the Eucharist is to bring about the communion of life between Jesus and the believer, the mutual immanence between God and us, which is entirely to our advantage. Merits, virtues, the love that is charity, and above all the Spirit of Christ — the Holy Spirit himself — become ours. We do not cease to be human persons. But it is God who, dwelling in us, makes us whole — that is, perfect in charity.

26
The Eucharist Is the Heart of Christ

"The Eucharist is the heart of Christ."[1] It is again Rajesh who reports these words of Carlo's.

We have already seen that all the liturgical actions of the Church make us contemporaneous to Christ: In the sacraments it is the Risen Christ who comes to us, who encounters us, forgives us, speaks to us, offers himself for us, enters into communion with us.

The Eucharist makes us contemporaneous to the passion, death, resurrection, and glorification of Jesus. These are the mysteries of his Passover. In them Jesus manifests and fulfills the will of love for the Father and for every human person of every era. For this reason, the Eucharist is also called the sacrament of charity.

Jesus, moreover, entrusting the Eucharist to his disciples, says, "This is my body which is given for you" (Lk 22:19; cf. 1 Cor 11:24). Even before the Passion, referring to this, Jesus had said, "No one takes [my life] from me, but I lay it down of my own accord. I have power to lay it down, and I have power to take it again; this charge I have received from my Father" (Jn 10:18).

He "loved his own who were in the world, he loved them to the end" (Jn 13:1): This is how the second part of the Gospel according to John opens, which deals with the Last Supper, the farewell discourse, and the events of his Passover. "He loved them to the end" is the key to understanding these facts, as well as the sacraments, which in a certain way make us contemporaneous with the effects of those facts.

In celebrating and participating in the Eucharist we are put in the presence of Jesus, who "loved them to the end" and today loves us to the end. The Eucharist accomplishes this self-donation of Jesus. And it is precisely this sublime love that is charity that allows Jesus to transform the infamous death on the cross into a free act that brings salvation to humanity.[2]

During car trips, Carlo and his mom used to listen to the catecheses on the sacraments given by my confrere Fr. Roberto Coggi, especially those on the Eucharist. They were so fascinated by them that they organized the transcription of the conferences to obtain a lively book: *Dialogo sull'Eucaristia. Incontrare, conoscere, amare Gesù "pane della vita."* In this text Father Coggi, commenting on this very "he loved them to the end" (Jn 13:1) reference, writes:

> That is, to the utmost limits of love. It is clear that with this verse the evangelist alludes to the institution of the Eucharist. He speaks of it in a "spiritual" way, according to his style, and thus completes the other evangelists, ushering us into the depths of the mystery. The Eucharist is therefore essentially a mystery of love.

In common speech the heart is often understood as the seat of the affections and of the most genuine love.

Therefore, Carlo links the Eucharist, which is the sacrament of the charity of Jesus Christ, to the heart.

27
We Will Increase Our Ability to Love

"Jesus is Love, and the more we nourish ourselves with him who makes himself food and drink for us through the Eucharist, which truly contains his Body, Blood, Soul, and Divinity, the more we will increase our capacity to love."[1]

It is his parents who report these words in their joint statement. In its content, this maxim of Carlo's recalls the passage of John 6:57: "As the living Father sent me, and I live because of the Father, so he who eats me will live because of me."

He who eats the Eucharist receives in his existence the ability to bring about the relationship of love that exists between Father and Son.

I will venture to explain John 6:57 in these terms: The Father, who is the origin of every good in life, eternally generates the Word. The Word is entirely in relationship with the Father. As a result, he who feeds on the Eucharist will be completely oriented to Christ and — because and as Christ is so to the Father — through Christ he will also be oriented to the Father:

> The Father-Son relationship generates the Son-believer relationship. … This means that every life, having its origin in the living Father, can exist only in communion with him, both in the Son and in the believer: this is then "dwelling" that from now on expresses the Father-Son relationship and the Son-believer relationship.[2]

Thus God himself increases our ability to live charity. Only God causes its increase. I cannot cause it to increase because charity is a divine, supernatural reality. I will only be able to ready myself for the increase. And attending Mass every day really means readying oneself for growth, for being oriented to Christ and to the Father.

Moreover, it must be remembered that in the celebration of Mass the Eucharistic prayer contains two epicleses — that is, two times the priest prays to the Father to send the Holy Spirit. The first time is over the bread and wine, that they may become the Body and Blood of Christ. And the second time is over those who participate in the Mass, that they, too, may be transformed — that is, that they may be one body and one spirit: "Grant that we, who are nourished by the Body and Blood of your Son and filled with his Holy Spirit, may become one body, one spirit in Christ."[3] The second invocation of the Spirit, the one over the participants, therefore has the aim of making us ever more, day after day, the living body of Christ, enlivened by his Spirit of love.

Carlo's words above bring to light his great penetration of the Eucharistic mystery. It is a penetration that did not arise from the study of theology; he was just a boy, a teenager. Rather, it arose from the love with which Carlo responded to Christ, from the exchange of love: Christ, loving him, gave him his Holy Spirit, who led him to all truth (cf. Jn 16:13), without strain or effort bringing him into the divine mystery.

The Eucharist has also been associated with a sort of heart transplant: It gives us the same ability to love as Christ, who gives us his Spirit of love.

28
We Are Beloved Disciples

"God creates all men as potential saints; it is up to us to carry out the unique and unrepeatable plan that God has always had in mind for each of us. We are all called to be, like John, beloved disciples, united with his Eucharistic heart."[1]

It is his parents who report these words in their joint statement. Carlo was always quite fascinated by St. John the Apostle, the beloved disciple, who at the Last Supper laid his head on Christ's chest (cf. Jn 13:25).

Carlo takes for granted the interpretation of the Church Fathers who identify the beloved disciple with the apostle John. Today this identification does not have many supporters. One of the leading scholars on this topic, Rudolf Schnackenburg, at the end of an extensive and thoroughly documented excursus concludes:

> The historically supported view that agrees with the internal evidence of John's Gospel is that the beloved disciple whom the editors identify with a long-lived disciple of the Lord may have been one of those venerable witnesses from the time of Jesus, whom the Johannine Church honored as their guarantor, bearer of tradition, and interpreter of the deeds and words of Jesus.[2]

Nonetheless, for Carlo the decisive question was not this. In the beloved disciple and in his gesture of laying his head on Jesus' chest, Carlo saw a clear message aimed at everyone: to become authentic and beloved disciples — that is, as his parents recall, "intimate friends of Christ." Carlo preferred the mystical interpretation, according to which the beloved disciple "is and represents the disciple perfected in faith and became an intimate of Jesus."[3] And the fact that the beloved disciple remains anonymous in the evangelical narrative means that each of us can identify with him. In fact, what loyal and sincere disciple is not beloved of Jesus, Master and Lord?

Moreover, John remarks twice on the position of the beloved disciple. This marking out is intentional and is in the image of the relationship of the Son, who is entirely turned toward the Father: John 1:18 uses the preposition *prós*, which signifies "a unique and permanent relationship,"[4] while John 13:23 uses the preposition én, "as if this position were momentary."[5] The beloved disciple has a relationship with Christ that draws on and is caused by Christ's relationship with the Father: The beloved disciple is a son of God, a participant in the same divine life precisely because he is within this relationship.

Finally, we have already recalled that Carlo identifies the Heart of Christ with the Eucharist. So, reclining the head on the Heart of Christ means being intimate friends of Christ through an intense Eucharistic life.[6]

29
Give Us This Day the Daily Eucharist, Too

"Jesus Christ became incarnate to come and save us both from the original sin inherited from our progenitors and from those that all of us commit every day, including involuntary ones, because unfortunately we are very limited, and the Eucharist is nothing other than the heavenly food to keep us from falling into temptation so often. Where the Our Father says, 'Give us this day our daily bread,' Jesus meant 'give us this day the daily Eucharist, too.'[1]

"O the depth of the riches and wisdom and knowledge of God!" (Rom 11:33): Who or what could lead a young kid to considerations of this kind? Was he mechanically repeating set phrases that he had heard? Those who recall his words for us attest that he certainly had an excellent memory, but that he was light years away from being stereotyped and artificial. Rather, they agree in remembering his ease of manner, originality, curiosity in reading, and liveliness of imagination.

Nor do we have any trouble recognizing in Carlo the result of the action of the gifts of the Holy Spirit. In particular, the gifts of understanding, which allows us to penetrate as if by intuition into the truths of God, and of wisdom, which allows us to savor, enjoy, and rejoice in God himself. These gifts are at the origin of Carlo's enthusiasm and originality.

"Give us this day the daily Eucharist, too": In one line Carlo concentrates the teaching of several ancient writers and Fathers of the Church who comment on the term "daily" in the Our Father (cf. Mt 6:11), which translates the Greek adjective *epioúsios*.

Origen translates *epioúsios* as "substantial." And so he teaches that it is

> the true bread, that which feeds the true man, made in the image of God, and he who feeds on it even becomes like the Creator. For the soul, what is more nourishing than the Word? For the mind that receives it, what is more precious than the wisdom of God? What has greater affinity with the rational nature than truth?[2]

Saint Cyprian, commenting on the Our Father, writes:

> Christ is the bread of life, and this bread is not everyone's, but ours alone. And just as we say *our Father*, since he is the father of those who understand and believe, so also we call it *our bread*, because Christ is the bread of us who attain to his body. We ask that this bread be granted to us every day, so that we who are in Christ and receive his Eucharist daily as the food of salvation may not be separated from the body of Christ in the event that a serious sin should intervene and therefore, deprived of communion, we be forbidden the heavenly bread, concerning which he preaches as follows: "I am the living bread that came down from heaven; whoever eats this bread will live forever; and the bread that I will give is my flesh for the life of the world" (Jn 6:51). … Therefore we pray that we be given every day our bread, that is, Christ, so that by abiding and living in Christ we may not distance ourselves from his sanctification and his body.[3]

And, finally, Saint Jerome interprets *epioúsios* in the sense that this is a "bread that is above every substance, that surpasses every created thing."[4]

30
The Lord Is There

"The Lord is there."[1] Various people testify that Carlo, going to church to pray in front of the tabernacle, would kneel down in one of the front pews, point to the tabernacle, and to anyone with him —Rajesh, his mother, Maria, or her nephew Ronnie (Carlo's age) — say with great simplicity, "The Lord is there."

"In the Eucharist Jesus is really present, and it is not a symbol"[2]: A few days after Carlo's first Communion, Sidi Perin, his confirmation sponsor, asked him, "What do you think, after the consecration is the host just a symbol that allows us to remember Jesus and the Last Supper?"

And Carlo replied, "In the Eucharist Jesus is really present with his Body, Blood, Soul, and Divinity, and it is not a symbol."

Sidi Perin immediately replied, "But when you eat the consecrated host it has the same taste, the same smell, the same color; how can it be the Body, Blood, Soul, and Divinity of Jesus?"

So Carlo began to explain the truth of transubstantiation: "The substance of the host, before the consecration, is the substance of bread, but after the consecration it becomes the substance of the Body, Blood, Soul, and Divinity of Jesus Christ, and the species of bread still remain the same even after the consecration, so their flavor, smell, and color do not change."

In the end Sidi asked, "But what is substance?" And Carlo answered, "The deepest essence."

31
Jerusalem Is Right at Our Doorstep

"Jerusalem is right at our doorstep."[1] So Rajesh testifies. But Carlo's mom also remembers these words:

> We are more fortunate than those who lived with Jesus two thousand years ago, because to find him and be close to him they had to move around continuously, while we have Jesus really present always with us; all it takes is to go to the nearest church. We have Jerusalem right at our doorstep.[2]

His dad once asked Carlo if he, too, wanted to take part in a pilgrimage to the Holy Land that was being organized by some priest friends. Carlo's response was disarming:

> I prefer to stay in Milan, because, anyway, there are church tabernacles where I can go visit Jesus any time, so I don't see the need to go to Jerusalem. If Jesus remains with us always, wherever there is a consecrated Host, what need is there to make the pilgrimage to Jerusalem to visit the places where Jesus lived two thousand years ago? Then the tabernacles should be visited with the same devotion.[3]

32
True Beauty

"Why are men so concerned about their physical beauty and not concerned about the beauty of their souls? The beauty of the body is like that of a rose; it lasts a short time and is destined to wither immediately." It is Antonia Salzano who reports these words from Carlo.[1]

Carlo compared external beauty to a sandcastle built on the beach: as soon as the first wave comes it is destroyed, and only a little sand remains. Spiritual beauty remains forever. Spiritual beauty consists in virtuous acts — in works of faith, hope, and, above all, charity toward God and mercy toward our neighbor. And it is nourished by constant and trusting prayer.

Carlo also said: "All efforts to stay forever aesthetically young and beautiful are totally useless. Anyway, everything passes. … What will truly make us beautiful in the eyes of God will only be the way in which we have loved him and how we have loved our brothers."

33
Lines and Lines

"There are endless lines to go see rock concerts or soccer games, and never a thought of lining up in front of the Blessed Sacrament."[1]

Carlo's irony is dramatically true. It is based on his faith in the real presence of Christ in the Sacrament. He was fascinated by the clarity with which Father Coggi speaks of this mystery:

> Mystery is not that which we cannot contemplate in any way, but it is that which always remains beyond our partial understanding. The mystery is that in which we never stop immersing ourselves. And wanting to immerse oneself in the mystery, despite knowing that it will always remain inexhaustible, is a sign of love. Theological investigation arises from love for the truths that the Faith proposes. ...
>
> What is present in the Eucharist is the same body that is in heaven, not another identical body. The body of the Lord is in no way reproduced, but only made present. That body of the Lord which is in the tabernacle is the same as that which is in heaven. All distance is eliminated.[2]

And the *Catechism of the Catholic Church*, which Carlo knew very well, teaches:

> In the most blessed sacrament of the Eucharist "the body and blood, together with the soul and divinity, of

> our Lord Jesus Christ and, therefore, the whole Christ is truly, really, and substantially contained." "This presence is called 'real' — by which is not intended to exclude the other types of presence as if they could not be 'real' too, but because it is presence in the fullest sense: that is to say, it is a substantial presence by which Christ, God and man, makes himself wholly and entirely present."[3]

It is paradise on earth.

34
Unbloody Sacrifice

"That sacrifice of the cross which took place two thousand years ago is made present again in an unbloody way in all the Masses that are celebrated every day. Like John, we, too, can associate ourselves with that same sacrifice of the Cross and thus show our love for God by taking part in holy Mass every day. We cannot ignore Jesus' call to unite ourselves with him."[1]

It is Carlo's parents who report this thought of his in their joint statement.

During the Last Supper and on Calvary, Jesus carries out the new liturgy of atonement and the liturgy of the New Covenant. "Jesus himself is the priest sent into the world by the Father; he himself is the sacrifice that is made present in the Eucharist of all times."[2]

Carlo's words are his internalization of what the *Catechism* teaches in a very succinct way:

> Because it is the memorial of Christ's Passover, the Eucharist is also a sacrifice. The sacrificial character of the Eucharist is manifested in the very words of institution: "This is my body which is given for you" and "This cup which is poured out for you is the New Covenant in my blood." In the Eucharist Christ gives us the very body which he gave up for us on the cross, the very blood which he "poured out for many for the forgiveness of sins."[3]

It is still just one sacrifice; that of Calvary is today made present in the Eucharist. Marie-Vincent Bernadot writes a sublime page:

> Now it is exactly the same liturgy that is reproduced among us on the altar: same priesthood, same priest, same victim, same immolation, same goal to be achieved. Only the outward form is changed: The Church triumphant celebrates the sacrifice in vision, the Church militant in faith. But there is only one liturgy. A marvelous concert rises every hour from the purified and sanctified creation toward the throne of the Almighty to bless him, exalt him, glorify him through the Lamb that is immolated; innumerable voices of the immense multitude of the redeemed are lifted up from all parts of the earth and heaven: but all these voices form but a single concert; they sing the one praise and celebrate the one liturgy.

This is why Jesus offered his sacrifice on Calvary and why he perpetuated his sacrifice through the Eucharist: so that *the praise of glory* may rise perpetually to God.

This is also the ultimate goal of Communion.[4]

35
The Consecration

"The decisive moment to ask the Lord for graces is that of the consecration, during the Eucharistic celebration, when the Lord Jesus Christ offers himself to the Father. Who can intercede for us more than God who offers himself to God?"[1]

The consecration corresponds to the Eucharistic prayer: from this moment, "the Eucharistic presence of Christ begins ... and endures as long as the Eucharistic species subsist."[2] Moreover, the Eucharistic prayer is for everyone, the Eucharistic sacrifice benefits everyone: "The whole Church is united with the offering and intercession of Christ."[3]

If we pay attention to the content of the different Eucharistic prayers, we can note that in every celebration of the Mass the Eucharist is offered for the pope, the local bishop, the priests, the deacons, the lay people, the living and the deceased, the children of God scattered everywhere. In a word: No one is excluded. Christ and the Church, his bride, desire to draw everyone to the Father.

For this reason "the decisive moment to ask the Lord for graces is that of the consecration."

36
Jesus Is Very Original

"Jesus is very original, because he hides in a piece of bread, and only God could do such an incredible thing."[1]

The Incarnation of the Word, and the sacraments that prolong its efficacy in the course of history, are a sign of the abasement of God on our behalf: "[Christ Jesus], though he was in the form of God, did not count equality with God a thing to be grasped, but emptied himself, taking the form of a servant" (Phil 2:6–7).

God, in his love, draws near to us and reveals himself without frightening us with his omnipotence; he proportions himself to us and to our condition, "abasing the infinite greatness of his divinity in order to adapt himself to the smallness of our mortal condition."[2] All the divine omnipotence is proportioned to our human condition, so that none of us may ever feel crushed or frightened, but always welcomed and loved:

> The action of divine love, although supernatural, is never accomplished in this life except through a sort of measure and gradualness proportioned to the condition of our present state. So, God shows its effects little by little and by degrees. In fact, if God wanted to hasten its wonderful fulfillment by realizing it all at one stroke with more liberality and with more abundance, without taking into account the way, form, and order suitable for drawing the spirit to himself, then it would be impossible for this spirit to bear the surges of the divine effusions. Therefore, during this sublime action in which di-

> vine love, like a penetrating fire, seems to consume and destroy everything within, the spirit that loves is compelled to invoke this powerful love with an impatient ardor and to beg it to put an end to its languor, promptly transforming it in the immense abyss of its most pure flames.[3]

It is a total abasement that makes man rich. And in the Eucharist the abasement of God uses bread and wine, the word and being gathered in community, which are common aspects of human life, precisely to enrich us with his own divine life.

37
The Victory

"The Eucharist manifests that the Church and the future of the human race are bound together in Christ and in no other reality. He is the one, truly lasting rock. Therefore, Christ's victory is the Christian people who believe, celebrate, and live the Eucharistic mystery."[1]

The passage just quoted is not from Carlo. It is an excerpt from the *instrumentum laboris* (the working document) of the 11th Ordinary General Assembly of the Synod of Bishops in 2005 dedicated to the Eucharist, source and summit of the life and mission of the Church.

Carlo excerpted this passage and copied it onto his computer, underlining it as if it were his motto or a theme to reflect on often. His parents saw this selection as his spiritual testament.[2]

38
To Thank Jesus

"To thank Jesus for the great gift he gives to men in making himself really present in the sacrament of the Eucharist."[1]

This is how Carlo responded when someone asked him why he was in the habit of doing a bit of Eucharistic adoration before or after Mass, as his spiritual father, Fr. Ilio Carrai, recalls it.

Carlo prepared for Mass by adoring, and after Mass he gave thanks by adoring. Adoration is the grateful and silent homage of our person, our intellect, and our love to God. And Eucharist literally means rendering thanks, thanksgiving. With silent adoration before the Eucharist our soul expands in praise and thanksgiving:

> [Christ's] life and his death have one goal that dominates all the others: first, to give God the most complete homage he could receive, and then to raise up in the world souls who, uniting themselves with his thought, with his love and his sacrifice, may render glory with him and be *the true worshipers in spirit and in truth* that the heavenly Father seeks (Jn 4:23). To adore and to form adorers.[2]

He who does not adore the Eucharist is like one who, after planting the seed, does not give it water so that it may sprout and grow more easily.

39
The Miracle of the Donkey of Rimini

"Certainly, the animal had been directly inspired by the Lord to confound the disbelief of most of the men, who surely would have preferred to dig into a nice big spread rather than worship the Lord."[1]

Carlo's words here refer to the Eucharistic miracle of Rimini, which occurred in Piazza Grande in 1227. Bonovillo, a Cathar, refused to believe that Communion was really the Body of Christ, and challenged St. Anthony of Padua, who was there to preach, with this proposal:

> I will keep one of my animals confined for three days and make it feel the torments of hunger. After three days I will take it out in public and show it the food all ready. You will stand across from it with what you maintain to be the Body of Christ. If the beast, neglecting the fodder, hastens to worship his God, I will share in the faith of your Church.

Saint Anthony accepted the challenge. And on the day appointed he arrived in Piazza Grande with the consecrated Host in the monstrance, while Bonovillo came leading his hungry mule.

Anthony asked the large crowd for silence and prayed: "By virtue and in the name of your Creator, whom I, however unworthy, hold in my hands, I say to you and order you: advance promptly and pay homage to the Lord with due respect." Immediately the mule, refusing the fodder in front of him, bent his forelegs before the Blessed Sacrament.[2]

40
The Sacred Heart of Jesus Is the Eucharist

"The Sacred Heart of Jesus is the Eucharist."[1] This is a saying that Carlo often repeated, as both parents report, and as proof he presented the Eucharistic miracle of Lanciano.

In Lanciano, at the church of St. Francis, fragments of the miracle are preserved. In the eighth century a priest monk, as soon as he pronounced the words of consecration during Mass, saw the bread become living flesh before his eyes and the wine become blood. With amazement he showed everything to those present. In 1971 and 1981, the remnants of this event were subjected to repeated microscopic and histological examinations. The fragments turn out to be human blood of the rare AB group, and human flesh of cardiac tissue.

As Dr. Franco Serafini has extensively documented, these same results are seen in the histological analyses of the remnants of the miracles of Buenos Aires (1992–96), Tixla (2006), and Legnika (2013).[2]

The Eucharist makes us present to the act of love with which Jesus offers himself to the Father. This act of love is the pinnacle of charity. Through the Sacrament, at Mass, the participants take part in this love. All of this is concretely and metaphorically signified by the heart, which in many cultures is traditionally the seat of the affections, the center of the person.

The prayer of the Church and in particular the prayers of the Mass for the solemnity of the Most Sacred Heart of Jesus refer to this truth. In the prayer over the offerings, reference is made to the "the surpassing charity in the Heart of your beloved Son," and the prayer after Communion says, "May this sacrament of charity, O Lord, make us fervent with the fire of holy love, so that, drawn always to your Son, we may learn to see him in our neighbor."[3]

41

He Who Criticizes the Church Criticizes Himself

"He who criticizes the Church criticizes himself."[1] It is Carlo's mom who recalls this incisive phrase.

The Church is that unity for which Jesus prays to the Father: "Holy Father, keep [my disciples] in your name, which you have given me, so that they may be one, even as we are [with the unity that makes us one]" (Jn 17:11; cf. 17:21–22).[2]

The New Testament uses two significant metaphors to express this unity. It is we who are built into the building that is the Church, like "living stones" (1 Pt 2:5; cf. Mt 16:18). It is we, as "members of his body" (Eph 5:30; cf. Rom 12:5; 1 Cor 6:15), who form the one body that is the Church.

If you want to reform the Church, start reforming yourself.

If you want a more credible Church, start being more of a believer yourself.

The New Testament also presents the Church to us with other metaphors: She is bride and she is mother.

Cardinal Giacomo Biffi pointedly said:

> The Church is for all of us a mother to be venerated, to be listened to, to be loved, not a wayward woman to be brought back to the right path, not an unruly daughter who enlightened Christians must take care to instruct and guide with their contrasting opinions. ... He who is unable to grasp the supernatural beauty of the Church demonstrates that he is unable to look at her with the

lovestruck eyes of Christ, and he cannot be a true herald of Christ because he is essentially too far from him.[3]

42
Confessing Sins

"Venial sins, too, must be confessed, because little sins can lead to committing mortal ones, and our world is full of temptations, and one must go to confession often to be in friendship with God."[1]

It is Umberto, Carlo's cousin and peer, who reports these words, together with the detail that "Carlo went to confession almost every week." Mattia, another of his peers, a playmate in Assisi, testifies of Carlo, "Every now and then he spoke to me about the importance of receiving Communion and told me to go to confession often."[2]

Frequent confession arises from faith in what is revealed in 1 John 1:8–10:

> If we say we have no sin, we deceive ourselves, and the truth is not in us. If we confess our sins, [Jesus] is faithful and just, and will forgive our sins and cleanse us from all unrighteousness. If we say we have not sinned, we make him a liar, and his word is not in us.

The explicit confession of one's faults is the indispensable condition for being able to enjoy the mercy and forgiveness that Jesus gives.

43
The Hot-Air Balloon

"For liftoff the hot-air balloon needs to unload its ballast, just as in order to rise up to heaven the soul needs to remove the small weights that are venial sins. If by chance there is a mortal sin, the soul falls back to the ground, and confession is like the fire that makes the hot-air balloon rise into the sky. One must go to confession often because the soul is very complex."[1]

"The smallest defect keeps us anchored to the ground in the same way that balloons are held down by the string held in the hand."[2]

The first statement is reproduced in the *Biographia Documentata*. Carlo probably used it when he taught catechism. The second statement is recalled by both parents, who omit the context.

These maxims reveal how aware Carlo was of the evil caused by sin, even venial sin: It is a fault that contradicts what God calls me to live. And he was also aware that the battle against evil is won in confession and in the sincere examination of conscience conducted in the presence of Jesus Christ, who is our *light* (cf. Jn 8:12).

44
Conversion

"Conversion is nothing other than turning the gaze from downward to upward. A simple movement of the eyes is enough": It is his mom, Antonia, who reports these words from Carlo.[1] And when he said it, his tone and gestures were half serious and half playful, pleasant and cheerful. He had the ability to communicate great Christian truths attractively and with expressive metaphors.

"Conversion is to stop plunging down and start rising up again. The lower down we have gone, the more difficult and tiring the climb back up will be. It will be important to reverse the course. Step by step, day after day, to move forward without ever stopping. The higher we climb, the more we will see things in the right perspective, in their entirety and totality. The higher we climb, the more we will enter the atmosphere surrounding co-eternity. We will breathe the air of the Infinite."

In order for his conversion to be sincere and constant, he had decided to go to confession frequently — that is, at least once every week.

45
If We Knew What Eternity Is

"If men knew what eternity is they would do all they could to change their lives."[1]

These words are from St. Jacinta of Fátima. Carlo knew them by heart and quoted them often.

Carlo was radically convinced that success in life is based on fidelity to God's grace: "If people truly realized the beauty of being in God's grace, respecting his commandments, they would do all they could to keep from committing grave sins and would exert themselves more to help those who live far from God."

It is entirely a question of love: In experiencing the limitless mercy that God has for us, we respond to this divine love with our love, which will not be solely human, but will be human-divine, because we are adopted children of God, participants in his divine life. And, always out of love and to spread this experience of joy, it will be natural to pray, desire, and work so that our friends may also take part in it.

This was the experience of Jesus' first disciples, Andrew and John (plausibly), recounted in the Gospel According to John (cf. 1:35–42).

46
Loving Others

"Happiness is in loving others as God loves them and not in venting on others one's own selfish desires."[1]

His mother, Antonia, remembers that Carlo said this to some of his close friends. The "venting on others one's own selfish desires" to which Carlo refers are acts or intentions contrary to temperance and chastity, like the use of pornography, autoeroticism, sexual relations between unmarried people, or even the exploitation of a spouse's body purely for the sake of release. Carlo understood that these attitudes are not authentic love, but forms of false love. Some still call them love, but they don't bring freedom or happiness, just bitterness and disappointment.

This is how the great signs of love, of the authentic kind that comes from God himself, are illustrated: "The fruit of the Spirit is love, joy, peace, patience, kindness, goodness, faithfulness, gentleness, self-control" (Gal 5:22).

47
Grave Sins

"If people truly realized the risk they run by contravening God's commandments, they would be much more careful not to commit grave sins and would exert themselves more to admonish their brothers who live in a way that is hardly in keeping with the baptism they have received."[1]

Sins are certainly contraventions — that is, transgressions of the divine law. But even more, they are infidelity to the love that God gives us, they are ingratitude, they are a failure of the plan of benevolence.

The inspired authors of the biblical books use many words to designate sin. The aspect that I find very significant is that the families of these words, in their main literal sense, mean "to miss the target," "to fail."[2] Sin is missing the target, it is straying from the path prescribed by Jahvé (cf. Dt 13:6, 11; Jos 7:11; Hos 6:7), it is failing the objective.

While the Ten Commandments let me know the goal, grace, and the new commandment of the love that is agape, they also bring me effective help in reaching it — that is, in being perfected in charity, as Jesus Christ is.[3]

48
The Outstretched Hands of Christ

"Priests are the outstretched hands of Christ. They must bear witness to the Lord with enthusiasm, and they themselves must be luminous models and not automatic repeaters of a liturgical rite into which they do not put their heart and from which their own faith in God does not shine through."[1]

It is Father Carrai, Carlo's spiritual director, who recalls these words. He had also noticed that Carlo was particularly sensitive to whether a priest celebrated Mass in a devout way, and if he realized that a particular priest was not very involved in the Eucharistic celebration he became sad.

"Priests are the outstretched hands of Christ": This expresses the truth in which the Church believes — namely, that the priest, in celebrating Mass or the other sacraments, acts *in persona Christi capitis* ("in the person of Christ the head"). Jesus Christ is the sole high priest of the new and eternal covenant, and he shares his priesthood with his disciples in two ways: in the baptismal or royal priesthood, and in the ministerial priesthood, which is at the service of the aforementioned priesthood. "The ministerial priest, by the sacred power he enjoys, teaches and rules the priestly people; acting in the person of Christ, he makes present the Eucharistic sacrifice, and offers it to God in the name of all the people."[2]

In the *Piccolo Catechismo Eucaristico*, which was part of Carlo's formation, Father Coggi clearly points out that, during the prayer of consecration:

The priest does not say, "This is the body of Jesus," but he says, "This is my body"; he does not say, "This is the blood of Jesus," but he says, "This is my blood." This means that the one who truly pronounces these words is Jesus. It is Jesus who consecrates the bread and the wine, making use of the priest who, so to speak, lends Jesus his mouth and his hands.[3]

49
Jesus and the Pope

"It was clearly Jesus who established the pope as head."[1] Carlo was about eight years old, and Sidi Perin, his confirmation sponsor, was testing his preparation in matters of faith by asking him trick questions: "Do you know that the pope is just an ordinary bishop like all the others?" By way of response, Carlo immediately cited the episode of Peter's confession in Caesarea Philippi, which is followed by the mission that Jesus entrusts to Peter:

> "You are Peter, and on this rock I will build my Church, and the gates of Hades shall not prevail against it. I will give you the keys of the kingdom of heaven, and whatever you bind on earth shall be bound in heaven, and whatever you loose on earth shall be loosed in heaven" (Mt 16:18–19). It was clearly Jesus who established the pope as head. The pope is the vicar of Christ on earth. If Jesus had meant that his successor was only Peter, the Church would have already come to an end. In fact, who would have ordained the other bishops and priests if Jesus had not given the mandate to Peter and his successors to do so?

At the age of eight, Carlo was able to retort with an effective argument, *from the contrary*.

50
The Heart of Jesus and the Heart of Mary

"The Heart of Jesus and the Heart of Mary are united."[1] Carlo said this to Rajesh, explaining to him the importance of the devotional practice of the nine first Fridays of the month, dedicated to the Sacred Heart of Jesus, and of the five first Saturdays of the month, dedicated to the Immaculate Heart of Mary. Carlo had been fascinated by the apparitions of the Sacred Heart to St. Margaret Mary Alacoque.

Devotion to the Sacred Heart had ripened his love for Jesus and stimulated him to make reparation for the sins of indifference toward God, sacrilege, and insult to the Eucharist. Carlo prayed and made reparation for these people and was seeking people willing to join him in this mission of love and fidelity to Christ. He officially consecrated himself to the Sacred Heart together with his parents and maternal grandma in Milan, at the church of San Fedele.[2]

Reparation is a theme that has almost disappeared, as if censored. Yet it is the logical consequence of the love that is charity: If I love a person, I will strive — as far as my possibilities allow — to remove not only everything that damages our relationship, but also everything that means infidelity to the will of the loved one. The love that is charity toward God drives me to make amends for my own infidelities and those of others, because I and the others constitute a single body, the Church.

The faith of Jesus' disciples is also manifested in the prayers of the Church. The collect of the Mass of the Most Sacred Heart of Jesus says:

> O God, who in the Heart of your Son, wounded by our sins, bestow on us in mercy the boundless treasures of your love, grant, we pray, that, in paying him the homage of our devotion, we may also offer worthy reparation.[3]

51
Always Close to My Heart

"So, Jesus and Our Lady, I will always have them close to my heart."[1]

Carlo was about four years old, and his mother had given him a gold necklace with a medal with the Sacred Heart of Jesus on one side and the Virgin Mary on the other. It was a gift that his great-grandma had given him four years earlier, on the occasion of his baptism.

Carlo was very happy to be able to wear the medal, and said contentedly, "So, Jesus and Our Lady, I will always have them close to my heart."

Thus he reveals his simple and sincere affection for Jesus and Jesus' mother, an affection that also led him to give kisses to a statue of Baby Jesus that had been given to him for Christmas.

52

If God Possesses Our Heart

"If God possesses our heart, then we will possess the infinite. He who trusts only in material goods and not in the Lord, it is as if he were living a life in reverse. He is like a driver who, instead of going straight and quickly toward his destination, [is] always going against traffic, in the direction opposite his goal, continually risking crashing into someone else."[1]

God begins to take possession of ourselves in a new way with faith and baptism, with grace and the life of charity. This is the beginning of divine life in us. We are possessed by the Infinite, and we possess ourselves, in the sense that we are admitted to taking part in the very life of the Trinity.

Carlo's words, recalled by his parents, seem to be an echo of Psalm 16:

> The LORD is my chosen portion and my cup,
>   you hold my lot.
> The lines have fallen for me in pleasant places;
>   yes, I have a goodly heritage
> Therefore my heart is glad, and my soul rejoices;
>   my body also dwells secure,
> For you do not give me up to Sheol,
>   or let your godly one see the Pit.
> You show me the path of life,
>   in your presence there is fulness of joy,
>   in your right hand are pleasures for evermore.
>
> (vv. 5–6, 9–11)

53
Infinity Our Goal

"Our goal must be the Infinite, not the finite."[1] We must recognize that Carlo had a remarkable clarity about the meaning of existence. This clarity came to him from his faith: In creating us, God at the same time calls us and orients us to himself — that is, to the blessed life of love and knowledge without limits. This orientation is like a sort of attraction and fascination. God draws us to himself, making us experience his mercy. Personal prayer, participation in the Eucharist, mutual charity, the works of the various virtues are all ways, complementary to one another, to live this experience of God's benevolence. No one is excluded. Many are distracted or misled.

Carlo did not let himself be distracted or misled;[2] he responded to this fascinating attraction.

54
The Only Woman in My Life

"Mary, the only woman in my life."[1] Carlo associated these words with what he considered the most chivalrous event of the day, the recitation of the Rosary. This is one of the ways in which he lived out his devotion and entrustment to Mary.

In 1996 his mom, the nanny Beata, and Carlo, who was five years old at the time, made a pilgrimage to the Shrine of Pompeii: On this occasion he asked to be able to take part in the special ceremony of entrustment to Our Lady of the Rosary.[2] This was his first act of entrustment to Our Lady of the Rosary of Pompeii; he would perform six more.[3]

In March 1997, Carlo, together with some friends, including Sidi Perin and Sergio Perin, consecrated himself to Our Lady at the church of Sant'Antonio in Milan, and in this way joined the Society of Mary Reparatrix.[4] As a reminder of this consecration he received a Miraculous Medal with a blue ribbon: Carlo considered it among the most precious things he had. He also infected his cousins in Rome with this devotion to Mary — they had come to Milan for the year-end holidays and Carlo invited them to make the same consecration to Mary at the Church of Sant'Antonio in Milan.

Mary certainly could not have been left out of Carlo's life. He knew that Mary, being the mother of Christ and our mother, takes it to heart that each of us should be in communion with Jesus Christ.

55
He Listens

"He listens and answers. But it takes belief, having faith that this dialogue is possible and real."[1]

It is Carlo's mom who reports this expression of her son regarding his prayers of petition. Carlo had filial confidence and firm trust that Jesus would listen to his prayers and his very desires, even the petition to admire a pod of dolphins in the sea. This is what happened in Santa Margherita Ligure in August 2006.

"No longer do I call you servants, for the servant does not know what his master is doing; but I have called you friends, for all that I have heard from my Father I have made known to you" (Jn 15:15). This is true for the first disciples, but also for today's disciples. Friendship always involves openness, availability, the commitment to obtain the authentic good of the friend and other goods that can lead to it. The friend desires and acts in such a way that his friend may grow and mature toward fullness of life.

56
I Come to Tell Jesus About Things

"Every now and then I come to tell Jesus about things."[1] Msgr. Gianfranco Poma had been at his new parish in Milan, Santa Maria Segreta, for just a few days. On the afternoon of July 2 or 3, 2000, he noticed a boy kneeling in prayer in a pew in front of the Blessed Sacrament. After a while the priest approached him, asked him his name, and then also why on earth he was there, and Carlo replied, "Every now and then I come to tell Jesus about things."

Carlo had just turned nine. This shows that he was already mature in the faith and that he had a bond with Jesus comparable to that which we have with brothers, sisters, or other close family members.

When we want to establish a bond with a person and then try to strengthen this bond, we arrange many opportunities to meet, talk, and share beautiful moments and lofty goals to achieve together. With his assiduous Eucharistic adoration, Carlo gives us the secret of his bond with Jesus.

57
If You Open Your Heart to God

"God is there for everyone. If you open your heart to him, he will open the way for you."[1]

Carlo said this to a friend, Vanessa, who was going through the pain of her parents' separation. He continued with these words: "Your parents will always love you anyway, even if they are separated because they didn't get along. If you open your heart to God and trust in him, he will help you find the way."

The theme of confiding in God returns, because opening the heart to someone means wanting to be in his confidence. And prayer is an act of trust in God that ends in filial abandonment to his will. "Trust in God, and he will help you; / hope in him, and he will make your ways straight" (Sir 2:6).

But there is another aspect. The opposite — that is, closing one's heart — means not loving, being indifferent without necessarily reaching the point of hatred. Therefore, opening the heart means not only confiding, but also loving the one in whom one confides. Prayer, a sign of theological hope, leads as if by the hand to love for God.

58
The Lord Will Let Me Know

"The Lord will let me know."[1] To those who asked him what he was going to be when he grew up, Carlo, with sobriety and without excluding any path, replied, "The Lord will let me know."

This is the sign, and also the result, of his prayer, confident in God. It expresses the firm and filial certainty of his hope: he already knows that God will not disappoint him.

These are words that do not convey anxiety, but deep serenity: "In returning and rest you shall be saved; / in quietness and in trust shall be your strength" (Is 30:15).

They are words that express Carlo's great freedom of spirit, because he knows that "if you intend and seek nothing else but the will of God and the good of your neighbor, you shall thoroughly enjoy inward liberty."[2]

59
Pray Very Much for Sinners

"Pray very much for sinners. Some of my classmates are far from Jesus."[1]

Carlo was ten years old and asking for prayers from the Poor Clares of the monastery of Vallegloria in Spello, in the province of Perugia. A cloistered nun, Sr. Luigina Consoli, remembers these words of Carlo's.

Carlo himself was in the habit of praying and interceding for others. His maternal grandmother, Luana, recalls, "After the TV news, he would recollect himself in prayer over some of the stories he had heard."[2]

Prayer in general, and intercessory prayer in particular, are acts that testify to the theological virtue of hope, the desire for our own conversion to Christ, and the desire for the conversion of our friends, the desire for the salvation of all.

Intercessory prayer for others assimilates us to Christ, who — as the Letter to the Hebrews says— "always lives to make intercession for them" (7:25).

It also makes us like the Spirit, the Paraclete, who "intercedes with sighs too deep for words ... for the saints according to the will of God" (Rom 8:26–27). And it is also a way of living the communion of holy things and fraternal charity, because we ask on behalf of others for the greatest good possible, communion with God in sanctifying grace.

The highest and most universal form of intercessory prayer is the Eucharistic celebration.

60
Our Prayers

"Even if one day it should happen to these kids, as they grow up, that they stray from the path that leads to God, sooner or later the Lord will remember the prayers they had recited together as a family and will bring them back to the fold."[1]

When he was about four years old, Carlo took the initiative to say bedtime prayers and asked his parents to pray with him. This act, done with insistence and simplicity, drove his parents to live their faith with new fervor and intensity. Carlo wanted his parents to pray with him, but also for all parents to pray with their children. If it is done attentively and with charity, and not with affectation or mechanically, this is a contagious way of living the faith and supporting one another.

Carlo also brings to light another important aspect: the merits of our prayers are never lost. This is the doctrine of the revival of the merits of our virtuous actions. The principle of supernatural merit is Christ and the charity that unites us with him. Being in God's grace, I perform a virtuous act, and this act, by reason of my communion with Christ, participates in supernatural merit. If, afterward, as Carlo says, "I stray from the path that leads to God" — that is, I sin, I lose communion with Christ — then I deaden the virtuous act performed before — that is, I keep myself from enjoying its fruits and eternal merit. But these virtuous acts remain present in God's sight. And when I repent and return to God, God revives for me his gifts which were my merits. This is alluded to in the parable referred to as that of the prodigal son: "The father said to his servants, 'Bring quickly the best robe, and put it on him; and put a ring on his hand, and shoes on his feet'"

(Lk 15:22).

St. Thomas Aquinas explains it this way:

> Meritorious works deadened by subsequent sin … [abide] in the Divine acceptance. Now, they abide thus, so far as they are concerned, even after they have been deadened by sin, because those works, according as they were done, will ever be acceptable to God and give joy to the saints, according to [Revelation] 3:11: "Hold fast that which thou hast, that no man take thy crown." That they fail in their efficacy to bring the man who did them to eternal life is due to the impediment of the supervening sin whereby he is become unworthy of eternal life. But this impediment is removed by penance, inasmuch as sins are taken away thereby. Hence it follows that deeds previously deadened recover through penance their efficacy in bringing him who did them to eternal life, and, in other words, they are revived. It is therefore evident that deadened works are revived by penance.[2]

61
He Is in Purgatory

"One day," Carlo told me, "I had the precise vision, lasting a precise, intense, and true instant, of my grandpa Antonio, who was asking for prayers because he was in purgatory."[1]

This is what Sidi Perin, the confirmation sponsor, testifies.

Carlo was very close to his grandpa, Antonio Salzano. They spent much of their summers together at the seaside near Palinuro, until, on April 29, 1995, Antonio suddenly died of a heart attack.

His mom, Antonia, recounts the same thing: "A few months after his grandpa died, Carlo said that he had seen him and he had asked for prayers because he was in purgatory, and after making his first Communion he was always looking for opportunities to dedicate indulgences and Masses for the deceased."[2]

Fr. Ilio Carrai also writes:

> He told me that in May 1995 his maternal grandpa, who had just died less than a month before, had appeared to him and asked him to pray because he was in purgatory.
>
> I believe that this episode increased his devotion to the souls of the deceased, for whom he often told me that he used to pray and offer indulgences and Masses.[3]

Luana, his maternal grandma, testifies that Carlo

> had a great deal of devotion to purgatory and offered Masses and prayers for the souls in purgatory. He also offered his Eucharistic adoration for the souls in pur-

> gatory. He also did the novena of St. Faustina, again for the salvation of the souls in purgatory. He got me to do it twice. It was a bit long.[4]

His parents recount that, as soon as he could, he earned indulgences to apply to the souls in purgatory. He liked to pray for them, especially for the most abandoned souls. Precisely to obtain the plenary indulgence for the deceased, when he was in Assisi he often went to Mass at the church of the Portiuncula, at which Our Lady and the angels had appeared to Saint Francis.[5]

62
I Saw Jesus

"I saw Jesus. He smiled at me and blessed me."[1] Again, his spiritual director, Fr. Ilio Carrai, writes in his statement of April 17, 2007:

> When he was six years old, a few months before making his first Communion, Carlo saw Jesus, who smiled at him and blessed him. Carlo was a deeply honest boy, so I considered his story plausible, but I tried not to make too much of it, to keep the boy from becoming too attached to these special graces, which are not important for the purposes of sanctity.

"Special grace not important for the purposes of sanctity": These are very wise words and full of discretion. The vision that Carlo received as a gift is certainly something extremely consoling and extraordinary. And Father Ilio was right not to give it weight, because as Louis Chardon, a theological expert concerning these phenomena, warns about these special graces: "Very often, instead of disposing man to union with God, they prevent man from progressing in it; indeed, they delay the encounter between God and man, and sometimes even go so far as to block it completely."[2]

In this existence it is more decisive to love God than to see him. Augustine succinctly says: "You do not see God. Love, and you possess him."[3]

63
The Rosary

"I remember that the Rosary was the daily prayer every night, so much so that it often happened that in the morning, when making the bed, he would find the rosary between the sheets, because he had fallen asleep while reciting it." These are the words of Beata, the nanny who lived with him in Milan for three years, from 1994 to 1997.[1]

"One of his favorite gifts for someone who came to his house was a set of rosary beads." This, again, is Beata's recollection.[2]

In February 2005, at the Grotto of Massabielle in Lourdes, he made a vow to Our Lady to always be faithful to the recitation of the Rosary.

Contrary to what it might seem on the surface, the Rosary is a simple way of praying, yet at the same time difficult. Simple, because you can pray the Rosary anywhere, because it consists of Our Fathers and Hail Marys, and the consideration of some of the mysteries of the life of Jesus. Difficult, because it always involves attentive meditation on these mysteries. The difficulty may decrease if you call your memory and imagination into play.

64
Is It All the Same?

"It's all the same, it's all the same, what changes?"[1] In the summer a relative had gone to Assisi to spend a few days with the Acutis family. After a while, she complained about the hikes in the mountains, saying that they were monotonous, the view was always the same. After that, when someone didn't appreciate the landscape, nature, or the sunset, Carlo, smiling, and in an ironic tone, would remind his parents: "It's all the same, it's all the same, what changes?"

Love for nature, amazement at the beauty of creation, wonder at its majesty were constant characteristics of Carlo. They were also translated into his care for creation, like the cleanup operations on Mount Subasio, removing broken glass and picnic trash, and in his earnest attention not only to his dogs and cats, but also to wild animals, like lizards.

65
It Doesn't Weigh on Me

"Come on, Vale, don't talk like that. It doesn't weigh on me to be around Andrea, because he's a great friend of mine, and I want to help him."[1]

This is how Carlo responded to Valentina, his grade school teacher. She often saw him with Andrea, a classmate with considerable personal, family, and academic difficulties. He also seemed like a pest. So the teacher, smiling, said to Carlo: "Come on, Carlo, give yourself a breather. Stay away from Andrea." But Carlo, instead of thinking of himself, calmly and joyfully thought of the good of his friend.

It was a great sign of fraternal charity, which "endures all things" (1 Cor 13:7) and leads us to "bear one another's burdens" (Gal 6:2).

Carlo's generous and accommodating friendship toward Andrea also continued through junior high. Ondina, a classmate in junior high, recalls, "In our class we had a mentally disabled kid who was often made fun of and ridiculed by many, but Carlo was always ready to defend him."[2] Without making a scene, Carlo stopped those who would have liked to bully Andrea. He did not tolerate injustices and abuses, so he always came to the defense of the other who risked being a victim.

66
I'll Gladly Come Give You a Hand

"How are you? Do your new students make you despair like we did? If you need help, tell me. I'll gladly come give you a hand."[1]

Carlo had moved on to junior high, and when he saw his grade school teacher, Valentina, he always greeted her cheerfully, and one time said those words to her. Carlo was aware that he enjoyed the esteem of his former teacher. He remembered — as she herself says — that she "used to put the most obnoxious classmates next to him during prayer services at school, and he was quite content to have them there, to keep an eye on them and encourage them to recollection," because, "certainly with his recollection, with his participation in the singing and the responses, he became an example."[2]

67
I Wasn't Hungry Today Anyway

"I wasn't hungry today anyway."[1] Carlo was generous with everyone. Some of his classmates in grade school were schemers and took advantage of his generosity by asking him for money to buy a snack. Carlo gave it to them and gave up having one himself. The teacher, Valentina, scolded the schemers and told Carlo not to do that. Carlo calmly defended his classmates, saying, "I wasn't hungry today anyway."

In a child of seven, such generosity is not a given. But also, not a given is the willingness to forgive the scheming of others.

68

Reaching Out to Someone Who Has Made a Mistake

"Adults sometimes make mistakes in their lives but don't realize it. And then we, being younger, must reach out to them. You may not understand these words very well now, but you will understand them better if you read the Bible."[1]

It is his friend Vanessa who reports these words that Carlo spoke to her. This teaching was a great help to Vanessa in forgiving her aunt.

Reaching out means that the one who loves takes the initiative, takes the first step, which also means forgiving. Being younger helps, because the youngster has no prejudices; he does not have the entanglements that complicate human relationships; he is simple.

The pinnacle of forgiveness is being able to justify the other who has made a mistake, as Jesus did, when, referring to his executioners, prayed on the cross, "Father, forgive them; for they know not what they do" (Lk 23:34).

69
He's Much Better than Me

"No. Carlo is much better than me."[1] Beata Sperczynska, who was Carlo's nanny until he was six, remembers that in first grade there was another Carlo, and this seemed to invite comparison. And one day Beata said to Carlo Acutis, "If you worked harder, you could be like Carlo." And he calmly replied, "No. Carlo is much better than me."

Envy and jealousy are thus ruled out, not that Beata wanted to prompt him to envy, but simply to virtuous emulation. Carlo was instead capable of recognizing the qualities and gifts of his classmates.

Carlo lived with the simplicity of a child, as well as what is said in Philippians 2:3: "In humility count others better than yourselves." When he grew up, he found confirmation of all this in *The Imitation of Christ*:

> It does not hurt to set yourself lower than all men, but it hurts exceedingly if you set yourself before even one man. Continual peace is with the humble, but in the heart of the proud is envy and frequent indignation.[2]

70
Humility

"Jesus wanted to set humility as the foundation of Christian asceticism. The humility that is also the foundation of the other virtue he preached so much: charity. Humility is the virtue that enables living in society, that brings together, that converts. What is humility? It is recognizing that everything I am comes from God. It is recognizing that all the good I have is from God. It is recognizing that the evil we have comes from us. The virtue of humility is a typically Christian virtue. He brought it to earth, living it first himself. Many say that Jesus was born poor, that he was placed in a manger … and owing to this he was born humble. But it is not owing to this that Jesus was born humble. Having united human nature with the divine nature was the act of the most sublime humility. This is why he could say, 'Learn from me, for I am meek and humble of heart.'"[1]

The clarity and depth of Carlo's faith are manifest here. To lay the foundation of humility he goes to the truth of the hypostatic union — that is, to the fact that with the Incarnation the eternal Word unites an individual human nature to himself.

71
The Light of Others

Antonia recounts that Carlo never made comparisons between himself and others, not because he considered himself above others out of pride, but because he was simple, modest; he preferred to keep a low profile; he absolutely didn't want to put himself on display. He once said to us, "Why diminish the light of others to make your own shine?": an expression that reveals how far he was from envy.

In the first year of high school he got a 9 on an essay. He got the highest grade in the class that day. Two of his classmates, who were considered the best in the class, had gotten a grade much lower than a 9 and were whining because Carlo had gotten a 9. Carlo, as surprised as he was by their reaction, told us that he had tried to console the two classmates and had told them that he didn't deserve the 9, and that the professor had graded him too highly.[1]

72
Sadness and Happiness

"Sadness is the gaze turned to oneself, and happiness is the gaze turned to God."[1]

His parents recognize that Carlo had a great ability to defuse situations, even the most difficult ones. They never heard him murmur, never complain, not even in the days close to his death. He always managed to be positive and optimistic and give confidence to others. Considering the concrete example of those who complain because they consider themselves unfortunate, of those who let themselves be gripped by depression and discouragement, Carlo said, "Sadness is the gaze turned to oneself, and happiness is the gaze turned to God."

The gaze turned to God is nothing other than faith. We can explain Carlo's maxim by referring some words of St. Catherine of Siena recorded in one of her many letters:

> I, Catherine, a useless servant of Jesus Christ, commend myself to you, comforting you in his precious blood, with the desire to see you a faithful servant before God, that is, that you be in that faith which gives joy and gladness to our soul. … O sweet, life-giving faith! If you are in this faith, sadness will never befall your heart. Because sadness does not proceed from anything other than the faith that we put in creatures, for creatures are dead and fleeting things that pass away, and our heart can never rest except in something stable and firm. … For today man is alive and tomorrow he is dead. So it is befitting, if we want to have repose, that we repose our soul, through

faith and love, in Christ crucified: then we will find our soul full of joy.[2]

73
You Can't Take It with You

"Think about the people who have nothing. You can't take it with you. It's better to be charitable."[1]

Carlo said this to his maternal grandma, Luana. And it is she herself who testifies to it. He was very frugal with himself. He didn't want his mom to spend money on him. And he didn't want his family members to splurge or buy unnecessary things. But rather than sacrifices as ends in themselves, these were always means to provide concrete help for the poor he met. His maternal grandma further recalls:

> In Assisi there were some homeless people who slept on the side of the road that leads to Via Santo Stefano. He would get me or his mom (depending on the time) to go with him and would leave them a sandwich and a five euro bill, both of which came out of his allowance.

Vanessa, too, his friend and playmate in Milan, says:

> When we went out for a walk together and he had his allowance with him, if he saw a poor person he would give without keeping anything for himself. He also did it with his toys: He gave many of them to me, who had none. He was happy and gave them to me with serenity, so there was never any act of self-superiority or humiliation of me. He made me feel like I was his true friend, and he was mine. He was a very simple guy who didn't demand anything, even though he could afford everything.[2]

74
I'm Interested

"I'm interested in the faith group that you presented."[1] It was the 2005–06 school year, and Carlo was attending the first year of classical high school, at the Istituto Leone XIII in Milan run by the Jesuit fathers. One of them gave a presentation to the incoming classes about an extracurricular group called the "Christian Life Community." Father Gazzaniga, a chaplain at Leone XIII, recalls that the only student who spoke up and showed real interest after the presentation was Carlo.

It is not enough to do charity; charity must be formed just as faith must be cultivated and formed. The proposal for an extracurricular group had precisely this aim: to give structure to the Christian life.

"He knew the *Catechism of the Catholic Church*, almost by heart, and explained it in such a brilliant way that he managed to get me enthusiastic about the importance of the sacraments."[2] This testimony is from Rajesh, the servant of the Acutis household, who was originally from Mauritius. He was Hindu and part of a Brahmin family, and recognizes that "it was precisely Carlo with his enthusiasm, with his explanations, with his films who brought forth in me the desire to become a Christian and ask for baptism."[3] Still, on the subject of Rajesh's baptism, Carlo's maternal grandma recalls that he wanted Rajesh to know Jesus. He absolutely did not want to force him, because he respected his freedom, but he ardently wanted him to ask for baptism, and when he received it, he was very happy.[4]

75
Get Him to Be Less Fanatical

"Lord, get Rajesh to be less fanatical."[1] It is Rajesh himself who recalls this detail: Carlo made a sign with these words on it, "because I was very attached to external things, to clothes, etc., and he wanted me not to be so dependent on those things." Carlo also prayed that Rajesh would not only be less attached to material things, but also less vain.

Carlo had been struck by the words that Jesus had spoken to Blessed Alexandrina Maria da Costa (1904–55) regarding vanity: "Through the vice of vanity men squander riches when these could feed many poor people."[2]

Carlo considered it vanity to go out dancing. His classmates would invite him, but he would politely decline the invitation. In this he was bucking the trend. He preferred something else, and above all something much better.

76
Like All Houses

"Like all houses, it has a living room, a kitchen, a bathroom."[1] Once Carlo had been invited to lunch at a friend's house, and when he got back, Rajesh immediately asked him what the house was like. Carlo, smiling, replied point blank, "Like all houses, it has a living room, a kitchen, a bathroom." So he gave no satisfaction to that vain curiosity, not only because he wanted Rajesh to be detached and to live a poverty of spirit, but also because Carlo was discreet and refrained from evaluating people — all of them, and even more so his friends — by the things they owned.

Curiosity is an excellent quality, a typical manifestation of the human intellect, which desires to know, seek out, and investigate what is necessary or useful, what is beautiful and lofty.

It becomes a fault when it is a disordered desire to know useless or unnecessary things, like wanting to know what does not concern us (such as others' private lives), or what goes beyond our common means of acquiring knowledge (and therefore resorting to illicit means by way of spiritualism, cards, demons), or what goes beyond the capabilities of our faculties, thus running the risk of making serious mistakes.[2]

Carlo's style recalls the teaching of Saint Augustine: "The soul, then, which purposes to keep itself chaste for God must refrain from the desire of vain knowledge like this."[3]

And also that of *The Imitation of Christ*:

> Cease from an inordinate desire of knowing, for therein is found much distraction and deceit. … And he is

very unwise, who is intent upon any things except those which avail for his salvation. …

We might enjoy much peace, if we would not busy ourselves with the words and deeds of other men, which pertain nothing to us. How can he abide long in peace, who thrusts himself into the cares of others, who seeks occasions abroad, who little or seldom recollects himself within his own breast?

Blessed are the single-hearted, for they shall enjoy much peace.[4]

77
Nobles

"Nobles in name are born so, they are not so by choice, there is no merit in being so. While nobles in spirit become so only by choice, and for this they will have many merits in heaven."[1]

It is Carlo's parents who report these words. Carlo was perfectly aware of the fortune and affluence of the family into which he was born, and he was likewise careful never to embarrass or humiliate any of those whom he helped. On the contrary, he thanked Jesus for the fact that he could share his allowance with those who were less fortunate.

"The greater you are, the more you must humble yourself; / so you will find favor with God" (Sir 3:18).

Thomas Aquinas, who himself came from the noble family of the counts of Aquino,[2] notes:

> In order that none should boast of the mere nobility of his blood and of his parents' wealth, Christ chose for himself parents who were poor and yet perfect in virtue. He led a poor life to teach disdain for riches. He lived in simplicity, without ostentation, in order to keep men away from the disordered craving for honors.[3]

78
I'll Take It to My Parents

"Thank you, Mirella, I'll take it to my parents."[1] Mirella is a businesswoman from Assisi and neighbor of the Acutis family. In 1998, having just gotten to know Carlo, she gave him some bread that she had made at home. Carlo took the bread, kissed it with joy, and said with intensity, "Thank you, Mirella, I'll take it to my parents."

In its brevity, this remark reveals many of Carlo's aspects. His immediate and spontaneous gratitude, his filial respect for his parents, and his levelheadedness and discretion, because Mirella, as she herself admits, would never have imagined the very prosperous social position of Carlo's family.

"Whoever honors his father atones for sins … and whoever glorifies his mother is like one who lays up treasure" (Sir 3:3–4). "With all your heart honor your father, / and do not forget the birth pangs of your mother. / Remember that through your parents you were born; / and what can you give back to them that equals their gift to you?" (Sir 7:27–28).

79
I'll Get My Dad, He'll Understand

"I'll get my dad, he'll understand."[1] Assisi, August 2005: Late in the morning, two nuns of the Congregation of the Lamb out begging for food knocked at the door of the Acutis home. Carlo opened the door for them, let them in, and said, "I'll get my dad, he'll understand." Carlo's dad testifies, "It was Carlo who didn't want to just give them food, but he asked me to invite them to lunch, and I did as he wished."[2]

Of this meeting Sr. Mariana Martin writes:

> We talked about our lives, and I was very much struck by Carlo's ability to listen, his joy, his peace in speaking and explaining things. We had, for example, talked about the fact that we had a problem with our computer. He got his and started looking for the solution; five minutes later he gave me the answer, and I was able to solve the problem we had been having for months.

This fact, too, reveals the hospitality, openness, and also the respect for paternal authority that Carlo lived.

80
Blind and Deluded

"All of us are deluded, because as soon as they tell us something not to our liking, right away we get angry."[1]

The delusion arises from the arrogance that blinds us to our defects:

> Oftentimes, too, we perceive not how great is our inward blindness. Oftentimes we do evil and excuse it. We are sometimes moved with passion, and we think it zeal. We reprehend small things in others and pass over our own greater matters (Mt 7:5). Quickly enough we feel and weigh what we suffer at the hands of others; but we mind not how much others suffer from us.[2]

Again, *The Imitation of Christ*, with great psychological penetration, notes:

> It is little enough that sometimes you should endure even words, since you have not yet the courage to bear hard stripes.
>
> And why do such small matters affect you? Because you are yet carnal (1 Cor 3:3), and regard men more than you ought. It is because you are afraid of being despised that you are unwilling to be reproved for faults and cover up with excuses. But look within and you shall acknowledge that the world is yet alive in you, and a vain desire to please men. For when you shrink from being abased and confounded for your failings, it is ev-

> ident … you are neither truly humble, nor truly dead to the world, nor is the world crucified to you (Gal 6:14).[3]

Certainly, fraternal correction is a rare art that must be practiced with the utmost fraternal charity before God.[4] And to be fruitful it requires that the one who receives it be humble and simple.

81
Being True Always Pays Off

"Being true and just always pays off."[1] It is Junio Massimo, Carlo's cousin, six months older, who recalls these words that Carlo repeated about purity and chastity.

Silvia, the mom of one of the classmates with whom Carlo often played, recalls:

> For him, chastity was true, and he was convinced of it, with no fear of proposing and living it. He was not afraid to express his beliefs in this area, regarding purity and premarital relations. He was convinced of the importance of purity also during the time of engagement, just as he was resolute in opposing abortion. I remember the discussions he had with my son and his classmates in the afternoons when they were together. They were not, therefore, convictions to be expressed only in public, but convictions rooted in the heart. That he was convinced in his heart is also demonstrated by the fact that he expressed his ideas with firmness and at the same time with respect, sometimes soft-pedaling to avoid an overly serious tone that might be irritating.[2]

Although Carlo was always respectful and calm, never priggish or patronizing,[3] these discussions caused him spiritual suffering and bitterness. He talked about this with Father Ilio, his spiritual director, who recalls:

> One time he was very upset that some of his schoolmates

> had expressed support for abortion, masturbation, and premarital sex, and he told me that he had met with many difficulties in arguing with these schoolmates and persuading them that it was not okay to behave this way. He often asked me for advice on how to help his friends act in accord with their own baptism.[4]

We will discover further on where and from whom Carlo got the ability and constancy to live in a sober, temperate, and chaste way.

82

Holy Temple or Fire-Eater's Puppets?

"A woman's body is like a holy temple."[1] It is Maria Gioia Pennino, his maternal grandma's sister, who reports these words of Carlo's.

His parents also recall, "He said that our body is the temple of the Holy Spirit, and he cared a lot about purity."[2] These words are evidently an echo of 1 Corinthians 6:15: "Your bodies are members of Christ."

Federico, a junior high classmate and Carlo's longtime friend, recalls:

> [For Carlo] premarital chastity was a value, even if it was clear to him that this involved commitment, discipline, a little effort. But it didn't seem to him that this effort should cost him too much, because the value of the girl's respect seemed to him too great to fall short of it. That he had values was evident. As for chastity, I have already said how important fidelity to the teachings of the Church was for him.
>
> I repeat that he was never vulgar in any of his expressions.[3]

Alessandra, a high school classmate and friend of Carlo's, writes:

> Carlo had very clear ideas about [what it meant] having a girlfriend; it mattered a lot to him, and he thought that

> respecting the girl was a very important thing. In fact, he told off friends of his who gave in to their boyfriends easily. He was a boy of great moral values and sound principles.[4]

Carlo's mother recalls:

> On more than one occasion I heard him on the phone lighting into friends who were getting ahead of themselves by having premarital experiences. In particular I remember that shortly before he died, again during the summer of 2006, the week his [paternal] grandparents had us out to the seaside, after dinner we sat out on the terrace to get some air, and he received a phone call from a friend. He got up and moved away so as not to disturb. But even without trying to hear it, their whole conversation was audible. I was struck by how Carlo spoke like a sage and lit into his friend, who had met a boy at a dance club and had immediately had intimate relations with him. He spent an hour explaining to her the dignity of the human person and the importance of remaining chaste. Since it was getting late … I finally ordered him to end the conversation. … Then I jokingly told him that even the girl's father should never have given her such a talking-to.[5]

His mom and dad remember that on several occasions Carlo reproved

> friends who visited off-limits sites, read things that he defined as harmful to the soul, or boasted of practicing autoeroticism. He told these friends that this was making them like the puppets in the book *Pinocchio*, where

Fire Eater used them for his shows and then threw them into the fire (his metaphorical way of illustrating what happens to souls that are unable to resist temptations and allow themselves to be led astray and overcome by their vices).[6]

83
It's Still Too Soon

"It's still too soon."[1] Valentina, his grade school teacher who continued to see Carlo, now in junior high, in the hallways of the same school, recalls:

> He was a very handsome boy, so sometimes I asked him to let me meet his girlfriend. Then he would blush shyly and with a smile tell me that it was still too soon. I liked to ask him this good-natured question because some of his classmates would introduce their girlfriends to me, while Carlo always showed me this beautiful respect for girls, that serenity of having to wait for the "right age" and of "it's still too soon," spoken with that blush that reveals modesty and clarity of heart. He wasn't timid or inhibited; he was a boy like all the rest, serene when it came to his affections.

Rajesh also confirms this:

> Another interesting thing about Carlo was his purity. He couldn't stand smutty images in advertising. He was a pure, fine boy, pure in his language, in his behavior. He didn't like it that someone his age should have a "little girlfriend," because he was convinced it was too soon. For this he was highly esteemed by his classmates, and he respected them very much. He always respected everyone, and very much.[2]

84
My True Love Is for Jesus

"My true love is for Jesus."[1] Here Carlo reveals the secret of his affections, the profound reason for his purity of spirit. His most deeply rooted affections and desires were for God, and God made him strong in temperance.

It is a friend of his, Vanessa, who reports these words:

> He was very respectful toward girls. As I said before, he never used the slightest vulgar expression. He was a calm guy, and he respected girls so much that this could be seen in his whole way of acting, so it wasn't possible to think that his thoughts were bad. And the girls looked at him, because he was a handsome boy. And he didn't take cover or shy away. He was, I repeat, calm, and he exuded so much serenity in his relationships with everyone, boys and girls, without distinction. He told me that the true love he felt was for Jesus. I remember it well: "My true love is for Jesus."

It is proper to the cardinal virtue of temperance and to that of chastity to know how to wait and to savor the time of waiting.

Carlo discovered that living charity toward God and neighbor with a spirit of gratitude is also a guarantee for living chastity. This is also what St. Catherine of Siena advised in one of her letters:

> Open the eye of your soul and see how great is the fire of the charity of God, who has sustained you until now and

has not commanded the earth to swallow you up, nor the brute animals to devour you. Rather, he has given you the earth with all its fruits, the sun, heat, light, the sky and its movement so that you may live; and a span of time that you may correct yourself. He has done all this solely out of love. Consider that, if you respond to this love, your soul and body, which are now like a sty, will become the temple in which God will delight to dwell with his grace. And then, when your life has ended, you will receive the eternal vision of God, where there will be life without death and contentment without trouble. May you not lose so much good for such a sad gratification.[2]

85
Killing of an Innocent

"Abortion is the killing of an innocent."[1] During his first year of high school a discussion flared up in class that many remember. Carlo made "a determined, generous stand, a resolute defense of the value of life from conception in the maternal womb.... He showed particular love and determination in wanting to persuade his classmates that in the face of the wonder of unborn life there cannot be sufficiently valid reasons to interrupt its development," as Fabrizio, the teacher present, recalls.[2]

Michele, Carlo's friend and classmate in grade school and junior high, also refers to an episode prior to his high school years, again a discussion between friends about abortion: "He defended the embryo in that it is a living human being and therefore a child of God."[3] This statement recalls Psalm 139:13–15: "You formed my inward parts; / you knitted me together in my mother's womb. / I praise you, for I am wonderfully made ... my frame was not hidden from you, / when I was being made in secret."

Maria Gabriella, the mother of Federico, Carlo's friend and classmate, remembers a discussion that took place at her house between the junior high kids on abortion:

> I had never heard Carlo talk about matters of faith, and I found the discussion striking. There was one boy in particular who said that the Church's positions were outdated, out of step with modern times. While the other boys were silent, perhaps because it was a discussion out of their depth, Carlo — in a way that struck me, given how firm and decisive he was — said clearly that it wasn't

> right, because it was still a murder. And he defended his position strenuously and to the end, without giving up or letting it go, or breaking off the discussion because it was too heated. I remember saying to myself: "This kid isn't superficial at all. He has very clear principles and values on which to base his life." And at that age it didn't seem like something ordinary to me, but special. I want to clarify that Carlo spoke firmly, but he wasn't being mean.[4]

His friend Michele also remembers a discussion between friends about same-sex couples: "He took a firm position against de facto couples not based on marriage, and especially not between a man and a woman. And I also picked up on his aversion toward adoptions by homosexual couples."[5]

86
Computer Scientist

"Computer scientist."[1] Carlo was six years old, wearing a white coat with a badge that displayed, "Computer scientist." One of his favorite games was to make believe he was a computer scientist. The game stimulated his natural predisposition, his extraordinary talent in this field.

"Really knowing how to use the computer also means being able to decipher the programs; otherwise, one is just an operator, not a programmer":[2] These words, too, come from Carlo. It is his friend Vanessa who recalls these words. She often took computer lessons from Carlo in the afternoon.

Carlo is remembered by many as "a computer genius." In this regard, Nicola Gori has edited a book that brings to light precisely these excellent qualities of his: *A Computer Genius in Heaven: Biography of the Servant of God Carlo Acutis.*[3]

87
Assisi

"Assisi is the place where I feel happiest."[1] Carlo spoke these words the last time he saw Fr. Ilio Carrai in Bologna. He says:

> Carlo told me that he had managed to achieve very positive results doing Eucharistic adoration. Carlo explained to me that he was finally able to no longer get distracted during Eucharistic adoration, and that thanks to it his love for the Lord had grown greatly. As he was saying goodbye he told me, "Assisi is the place where I feel happiest."

Certainly, this was partly so because Assisi was the usual family vacation spot. But just as certainly for the simple and essential tenor of the life he led there. He enjoyed swimming in the pool with his friends Jacopo and Mattia, or going with them to the woods along with his parents and their dogs. He enjoyed running in the fields and shooting videos with his friends.

He dedicated himself to music and in to playing the saxophone.

He would climb Mount Subasio and admire the places first associated with St. Francis: the convent of Rivotorto, St. Mary of the Angels, and San Damiano. More than once a week he went to Mass or to pray at the Basilica of Saint Francis. He spent a lot of time there, going to confession and then praying at the tomb of Saint Francis, savoring the peace and joy that Francis too had known.

88
Fátima

"If Francesco, who was so worthy, so good and simple, had to recite many Rosaries to go to paradise, how can I make myself deserving of it, when I am so much less holy than him?"[1]

February 2006: The Acutis family was on a pilgrimage to Fátima. Everyone had prepared for the pilgrimage, in part by reading the *Diary* of Sister Lucia (one of the seers as a child).

At the shrine they were welcomed by Sr. Maria João Marquès Antes and Sr. Angela Codeluppilo, who told them of the meaning and content of Our Lady's apparitions, the lives of the three children, and the apparitions of the angel of Portugal that preceded those of Our Lady.

When they came to the episode in which the three children asked Our Lady if they, too, would be taken to heaven, Carlo was troubled by the answer they received: Lucia and Jacinta, surely, while Francesco would have to recite many Rosaries to be taken to paradise.

So, Carlo asked his parents, "If Francesco, who was so worthy, so good and simple, had to recite many Rosaries to go to paradise, how can I make myself deserving of it, when I am so much less holy than him?"

Carlo asked his parents many questions, and even more when he read the account of the vision of hell. From all this he drew a resolution: to intensify his prayers for those in danger of losing their souls for eternity.

89
Hell

"If souls are truly in danger of damnation, I don't understand why today there's almost no talk of hell."[1]

Carlo was well aware of the Church's teaching on the four last things — that is, on the ultimate realities which are death, judgment, hell, and paradise. He became excited when speaking with anyone about Jesus, the saints, and paradise.

His passion for proclaiming salvation drove him to create an exhibit on Eucharistic miracles. Once this was finished, he started planning a display on hell, purgatory, and paradise. He talked about these ultimate realities with his friends. Some of them made fun of him precisely because he believed in them. Despite this Carlo continued to testify to his faith with enthusiasm and serenity. Indeed, he planned exhibitions that would come to light after his death, and he prayed for those who lived in indifference.

Carlo was aware of this teaching in *The Imitation of Christ*:

> If you oftener think of death (Eccl 7:1,2) than of living long, there is no question but you would be more zealous to amend. If also you considered the penalties that are to be in hell (Mt 25:4), I believe you would willingly undergo labor and sorrow, and not be afraid of the greatest austerity. But because these things do not enter your heart, and you still love those things which flatter, therefore you remain cold and very sluggish.[2]

90
I've Put on Seventy Kilos

"I've put on seventy kilos, and I'm destined to die."[1] July 2006: Carlo's voice is recorded on a video he made in which he is waving and smiling. His parents found this video on his computer only after Carlo's death.[2]

Carlo could be referring to the transience of his earthly existence, to the vanity of his human body, which, as much as it may have grown in beauty and vigor, was still destined for death.

And it could also be a premonition of the death that would overtake him in a few months.

His parents recall:

> Ever since he was a child he said that he would die of a broken vein, which in fact happened, because the cause of death was a cerebral hemorrhage. And when he got sick he weighed exactly seventy kilos. In the past, some episodes had already happened in which he had said things without realizing that afterward they came true.[3]

"You know, I won't live long":[4] It is his maternal grandmother, Luana, who recalls these words. "Carlo often said them to the servant, Rajesh," she said. "They are words that always made an impression on me."

They would therefore seem to be a premonition.

The video and the statements do not reveal fear, but rather a great sense of serenity and peace. In *The Imitation of Christ*, which Carlo loved to meditate on, it is written:

> "All is vanity" (Eccl 1:2), but to love God and to serve him only. For he who loves God with all his heart is neither afraid of death, nor punishment, nor of judgment, nor of hell; for perfect love gives secure access to God (Rom 8:39). But he who delights still to sin, what marvel is it if he fears both death and judgment? Yet it is good, although love be not forceful enough to call you back from sin, that at least the fear of hell should restrain you.[5]

Carlo's serenity is explained by his conviction: "I am doing well as long as God accompanies me every day of my life. If he accompanies us, we are always doing well."[6]

September 2006: Vanessa's mom was ironing in the Acutis house; Carlo came up and hugged her. She asked him how he was doing, and Carlo answered with those words. No one would ever have imagined that in about fifteen days Carlo would have to be urgently admitted to the hospital.

91
The Lord Has Given Me a Wake-Up Call

"The Lord has given me a wake-up call."[1] Carlo reacted with these words to the diagnosis he had just been given: acute leukemia, type M3. His grandma, who was there, remembers that he said this with an arresting serenity. His mom recalls that when he said it, he was smiling.

"Mom, remember that I'm not getting out of here alive."[2]

By this time Carlo was hospitalized at San Gerardo in Monza. His parents and maternal grandmother were there with him.

"Grandma, I guess this time I'm not going to make it."[3]

The serenity and peace with which Carlo lived these last days were the perceptible signs that he was experiencing the bliss of divine consolation: "Blessed are those who mourn, for they shall be comforted" (Mt 5:4).

"Sorrowful, yet always rejoicing," Saint Paul writes in 2 Corinthians 6:10. Carlo was experiencing the acute and lethal illness — he knew this perfectly well — and he was consoled by God. The consolation he received did not take away the cause of his affliction. But it made the affliction a condition of bliss. His affliction was transfigured: "The law of Christian life is a law of transfiguration, and not of substitution."[4]

92
There Are People Who Suffer More Than Me

"There are people who suffer more than me."[1] A doctor from the Monza hospital asked him if he was suffering, and with a smile Carlo replied, "There are people who suffer more than me." All of the nurses and doctors were amazed at his gentleness; he smiled at everyone as if he wanted to reassure them. He did nothing but apologize to the nurses for the hard work they had to do on account of his illness, and when they tended to him, he tried with the very little strength he had to go from the bed to the gurney on his own just to make their work easier.

Andrea Acutis remembers this of those hours:

> Of course, we saw that the nurses [of the San Gerardo hospital in Monza] were worried, but I still couldn't manage to think that he was dying. Carlo had a moment of agitation, and he apologized, thinking that he was causing concern with his reaction, which lasted a few seconds. Otherwise, what struck me was Carlo's serenity: not one complaint, despite being intubated and full of needles.[2]

Even half an hour before going into a coma, he maintained his serenity and his desire not to burden others. Everyone got the impression of having before him a special kid who did not want to show his suffering or be a bother. Even in these circumstances he was able to inspire confidence.[3]

93
I'm Heading for Peace

"The ways of the Lord are infinite. I'm heading for peace. The happiness I'm heading for is not of this life."[1]

Vanessa would have liked to go and visit Carlo in the hospital. But given such a serious clinical picture, it was not possible. So she, together with her Uncle Rajesh, called his mom, Antonia, several times to get news, and on these occasions Antonia said that Carlo was very calm and had spoken those words.

94
Passing on to Co-Eternity

"Down here we do not have a stable city, but we are seeking the future one. We have been elevated to supernatural status, redeemed and saved; we are destined for eternity with God, 'co-eternity.' Death is not the finale of everything. It is not the end. It is not ruin. It is not the fatal conclusion. It is the passage to co-eternity. If we consider ourselves to be passing through this world, if we conduct ourselves like sojourners, if we aspire to the things above, if we configure everything on the hereafter, if we base our existence on the beyond, then everything is ordered, everything is balanced, everything is oriented, everything is substantiated by hope."[1]

It is Antonia who remembers how Carlo would say these things to his best friends.

Existence is already a fleeting passage. And death itself is a passage. They are two aspects of Pascha, which means passage. And if eternity indicates a quality of God — that is, being not in time but in a life that does not know the succession of before and after, a life that is the simultaneous fullness of joy and love — then co-eternity indicates our participation in this overflowing condition.

95
Alexander Sauli

On January 1, 2006, at the drawing of the protector saint of the year, Carlo received the holy card of St. Alexander Sauli.

On October 8, 2006, as soon as Carlo was admitted to the Clinica De Marchi, his mom and maternal grandma went to Mass at the church across from the hospital. It is a church of the Barnabites, and in it the mortal remains of St. Alexander Sauli are preserved.[1]

St. Alexander Sauli died on October 11.

Carlo died on October 11, 2006.

There is no such thing as coincidence. It is rather — as we have already seen — "the disguise God has chosen so as to walk among us while remaining incognito,"[2] and not frighten us with his omnipotent benevolence.

We are all part of a divine plan of providence.

96
I Offer to the Lord

"Everything I am suffering I offer to the Lord."[1] It is Rajesh who remembers these words. Carlo was living out his last days. It was October 4,[2] and he was still at home in Milan. But his situation was gravely deteriorating. And he knew it.

"I offer my life for the pope, for the Church, so as not to go to purgatory and go straight to paradise."[3] It is his grandma Luana who reports both Carlo's words and her reaction: "I commented with, 'Oh my,' as if to say, 'he's exaggerating just a bit.'"

His parents also testify to these words in their deposition.[4]

Living life as an offering of oneself to God and one's brothers is the pinnacle of the love that is charity.

All the facts of the redemptive Incarnation of Jesus can be read in the light of self-sacrificing love — that is, the love that makes a total gift of self: "The Son of Man also came not to be served but to serve, and to give his life as a ransom for many" (Mk 10:45). "I am the good shepherd. The good shepherd lays down his life for the sheep" (Jn 10:11; cf. 10:15,17).[5]

Moreover, the proper names with which we designate the Holy Spirit are Love and Gift[6]: The Holy Spirit is the Love that proceeds from the Father and the Word is a pure and free Gift. In his farewell discourse Jesus says, "I will ask the Father, and he will give you another Counselor, to be with you for ever, even the Spirit of truth … for he dwells with you, and will be in you" (Jn 14:16–17). The Spirit is given to us to remain always with us, to dwell in us and communicate to us the life of supernatural love, to elevate our love to an oblative love, to an offering of thanksgiving.[7]

Frequent in the Eucharistic liturgy are prayers in which we

are called on to make our existence an offering pleasing to God. I will recall just two as examples: "As we honor the memory of the Mother of your Son, we pray, O Lord, that the oblation of this sacrifice may, by your grace, make of us an eternal offering to you.[8] And in Eucharistic Prayer III, the second epiclesis has these words: "May he make of us an eternal offering to you, so that we may obtain an inheritance with your elect."[9]

97
Lamb

The lamb was present at some of the most important events in Carlo's life — for example, a lamb-shaped cake. To celebrate the baptism of little Carlo, his mom asked a trusted pastry chef to prepare a lamb-shaped cake. Antonia was not practicing the Faith, but she knew the many symbolic meanings of the lamb.

It is the lamb of the exodus from Egypt that saves Israel (Ex 12:1–14). It is the not yet fully grown member of the flock that is offered daily in sacrifice in the Temple of Jerusalem. It is the suffering Servant of Jahvé prophesied by Isaiah 53:7: "Like a lamb that is led to the slaughter / and like a sheep that before its shearers is silent, / so he opened his mouth" — and realized in Jesus Christ through his passion and death. John the Baptist presents Jesus to his disciples as the lamb of God: "Behold, the Lamb of God, who takes away the sin of the world" (Jn 1:29). The deacon Philip recognizes in Jesus the lamb prophesied by Isaiah (see Acts 8:26–33), as does 1 Peter 1:18–19: "You were ransomed … with the precious blood of Christ, like that of a lamb without blemish or spot."

Antonia, with this highly symbolic gesture, wanted to thank God for the gift of Carlo, and she entrusted it, she presented it to God so that in God it might be an instrument of salvation.[1]

A few months later his parents gave little Carlo a stuffed animal, a little lamb with white fur. Carlo became very fond of this plush toy and "even when he grew up, he kept it, because it reminded him of Jesus."[2]

On June 16, 1998, going to first Communion, they were in the car heading for Perego, to the monastery of the hermit nuns of St. Ambrose. Suddenly a little white lamb crossed the road leading up to the hill. Then the shepherd and other sheep followed. Carlo smiled when he saw these animals, but especially the little white lamb, and he told his parents that it seemed to him like a little sign sent by the Lord as a gift.

At the end of Carlo's very rapid illness his father remembers him like this: "To me he seemed like a lamb that makes no moan: not a tantrum, not a complaint, just kindness with everyone, the medical and nursing staff and all of us. And yet with the awareness that he was dying."[3]

Finally, the Revelation of John, in speaking of Jesus, dead and now gloriously risen, favors the image of the lamb. Jesus is the Lamb that is "standing" — that is, he is alive and risen — "as though it had been slain" — that is, he has the marks of his passion — "at the right hand of him who seated on the throne" (Rv 5:6) — that is, he is at the right hand of God the Father and shares in his glory and omnipotence. Jesus is the Lamb that receives "honor and glory" from all creatures (see 5:6–14) and is the only one able to open the "seven seals" — that is, to fulfill perfectly the universal plan of salvation. He is the Lamb that leads the elect to the springs of the waters of life (7:17). Jesus is the Lamb that conquers and leads to victory those who are with him (17:14). The Lamb is the "temple" of the heavenly Jerusalem (21:22), he is the "lamp" that illuminates it (21:23). From his throne flows a "river of the water of life, bright as crystal" (22:1), which is the Holy Spirit. The Lamb is the bridegroom of the holy city, of the heavenly Jerusalem (21:9) — that is, he is the complete Love that is the goal and reward of the saints.

During his life, Carlo encountered the lamb several times in its symbolism. Now Carlo is with the Lamb in his substantial reality — that is, he participates in the wedding of the Lamb sacrificed for us from the creation of the world.

98
Kit for Becoming Saints

For a few years Carlo taught catechism at his parish in Milan. He had proposed to the children the goal of becoming saints. So, he had come up with a kit for becoming saints:

> I want to let you in on some of my very special secrets that will help you quickly reach the goal of sanctity. Always remember that you, too, could become a saint! First, you must desire it with all your heart, and if you don't yet want it, you must ask the Lord for this insistently.
>
> 1) Try to go to Mass every day and receive holy Communion.
> 2) If you can, spend a few moments in Eucharistic adoration in front of the tabernacle where Jesus is really present, and you will see how your level of holiness will increase!
> 3) Remember to recite the holy Rosary every day.
> 4) Read a passage of Sacred Scripture every day.
> 5) If you can, make a confession every week, also of venial sins.
> 6) Often make resolutions and little sacrifices to the Lord and Our Lady to help others.
> 7) Ask for help from your guardian angel, who must become your best friend.[1]

99
"Fervid Fantasy" and "Revelatory Silence"

Here are two poems written by Carlo.

Fervid Fantasy
Fervid fantasy
I don't know who you may be
just don't lead me to the illusion
of a life made of fiction.

Revelatory Silence [literal translation]
Revelatory silence
like a hissing snake,
you, you subdue people
like a shadow of terror,
you, you terrify every lover;
appearance!
to him who listens to you
you are like fresh grass plucked
that refreshes the mind
and at the same time doesn't lie

Silence, the Revelator [loose translation]
Silence, the revelator,
like a sibilant viper
you, you make people cower

at your shadow of terror,
you, you terrify every lover;
appearance!
to him who heeds your word
you are like fresh grass upgathered
that refreshes the mind
and is not the lying kind.

100
“Vain Hope” and “Lurid Distraction”

Here are two more poems written by Carlo.

Vain Hope [literal]
Vain hope,
Poisoned apple with pleasant semblance;
he who has eaten you,
like a mole,
wanders frightened in the tunnels;
breaking the ropes of the harp
that support the boat,
on the water suspended
it sinks without surprise.

Vain Hope [loose]
Hope in what is vain,
poisoned apple with lovely skin;
he who makes you his bite
wanders mole-fashion out
into the tunnels, in fright;
breaking the strings of the boat
that keep it afloat,
let down on the water,
no surprise — it goes under.

Lurid Distraction [literal]
Lurid distraction,
you seem an emotion,
but by now,
I know you well;
you live in the woods
apparently enchanted,
but clearly fabricated.
Just to avoid you,
because I myself
am your accomplice,
takes running aground;
But then, great victory,
it seems almost a story
but it's reality
already become history.

Lurid Distraction [loose]
Lurid distraction,
You seem like an emotion,
but by now
I know your every move;
you live in the grove
apparently enchanted,
but clearly fabricated.
Just to sidestep you,
because I myself abet you,
I have to go to ground;
but then, great victory,
it seems almost a story
but it's reality
already gone down in history.

Conclusion

As a conclusion, a passage from the Letter to the Hebrews immediately came to mind:

> Therefore, since we are surrounded by so great a cloud of witnesses, let us lay aside every weight, and sin which clings so closely, and let us run with perseverance the race that is set before us, looking to Jesus the pioneer and perfecter of our faith. (12:1–2)

"Surrounded by so great a cloud of witnesses": The testimony of our brothers in faith is of capital importance for our growth in faith and charity. They are not only an example to imitate, because Christianity is not simply a morally good life, but they are our companions in existence, our intercessors, our guides under the one head who is Jesus Christ, our benefactors, because in the communion of holy things they pass their merits on to us. Carlo was fascinated by the lives of many witnesses, of many saints. Now he himself is our witness.

"Let us lay aside every weight, and sin which clings so closely": From the testimonies of those who knew him, it seems that Carlo always lived in the grace of God — that is, that he did not commit grave sins. So, he bears witness to us of one fact: It is possible today to live in harmony with the will of God.

Let us "run with perseverance the race that is set before us": Carlo's life was a race, fast and brief. He has reached the goal he longed for.

"Looking to Jesus the pioneer and perfecter of our faith": Carlo — we have seen this repeatedly — always desired and concretely lived communion with Jesus, in many ways, in the simplest prayer, in silent meditation, in the Eucharist, in fraternal friendships. Jesus Christ took hold of him. And Carlo let himself be vanquished.

Notes

Introduction

1. Since May 27, 2006, other Eucharistic miracles have been documented: in Tixla, Mexico, in 2006; in Sokólka, Poland, in 2008; and in Legnica, also in Poland, in 2013. On all these quite recent miracles, I refer to the book that is by far the most thoroughly documented from the medical-scientific point of view: Franco Serafini, *Un cardiologo visita Gesù*, ESD, 2nd edition, Bologna, 2020.

2. *I miracoli eucaristici e le radici cristiane dell'Europa*. This text has gone into its third edition, revised and expanded, ESD, Bologna, 2014. Two authors appear on the cover: Sergio Meloni and Istituto San Clemente. In reality, Carlo's valuable contribution is hidden behind the name "Istituto San Clemente."

3. Francis, post-synodal apostolic exhortation to young people and to the entire people of God *Christus Vivit*, March 25, 2019, Nos.104–106.

4. Congregatio de Causis Sanctorum, *Mediolanensis Beatificationis et canonizationis Servi Dei Caroli Acutis, Christifidelis Laici (1991–2006) Positio super vita, virtutibus et fama sanctitatis*, Romae, 2017. In particular, the *Summarium Testitum* includes pp. 93–340. The *Declarationes* are on pp. 341–393. Of great use for reconstructing the context of Carlo's life is the *Biographia Documentata*, pp. 395–624, at the end of which Carlo's poems and some of his other writings are also reproduced.

Chapter 1: First Steps in the Faith

1. *Positio*, 295. Notes containing nothing but a number refer to the page number in the *positio*.

2. 295.

3. Cf. Pietro Ferrandi, *Legenda di San Domenico*, 5–6, cited in P. Lippini, *San Domenico visto dai suoi contemporanei*, ESD, Bologna,

1998, 73; and in G. Festa, A. Laffay, *San Domenico. Padre dei Predicatori*, ESD, Bologna, 2021, 250–253.

Chapter 2: We Are All Born as Originals ...

1. 292.

2. Francis, *Christus Vivit*, No. 105.

3. C. Caffarra, *Prediche corte, tagliatelle lunghe*, ESD, Bologna, 2017, 15–16.

4. 305.

5. 305.

6. 285.

Chapter 3: God Is Always with Us ...

1. 313.

2. Cf. A.-M. Besnard, *Le mystère du Nom*, Cerf, Paris, 1962.

3. J. Gnilka, *Il Vangelo di Matteo*, Parte seconda, Paideia, Brescia, 1991, 743.

4. G. Barzaghi, *Lo sguardo della sofferenza*, ESD, Bologna, 2011, 84.

5. Cf. G. M. Carbone, *Ma la più grande di tutte è la carità*, 2nd ed., ESD, Bologna, 2020, 85; G. Nebe, Πολυς, in H. Balz, G. Schneider, *Dizionario esegetico del Nuovo Testamento*, Paideia, Brescia, 1998, 2, 1049.

Chapter 4: You Don't See God. But He Sees You ...

1. 174.

2. 174.

3. G. Biffi, *Homily on the occasion of his eightieth birthday*, given in Bologna at the Shrine of Our Lady of San Luca, June 13, 2008.

Chapter 5: Not I, but God

1. 291 and 324.

2. 291.

3. Raymond of Capua, *Legenda maior, Vita di santa Caterina da Siena*, I, ch. 10, No. 95, Cantagalli, Siena, 1985, 110.

4. 270–271.

5. 276.

6. 279.

Chapter 6: Not Self-Love, but the Glory of God

1. 324.

2. 291 and 324.

3. Thomas à Kempis, *The Imitation of Christ*, I, 7, 2, Whitaker House, Springdale, Pennsylvania, 1975.

Chapter 7: Every Minute That Goes By …

1. 303.

2. *The Imitation of Christ*, I, 25, 11.

3. *The Imitation of Christ*, I, 18, 2–3.

4. 137.

Chapter 8: That God May Make Me Become a Saint

1. 371.

Chapter 9: A Gift So Great

1. 291.

2. 291.

Chapter 10: To Send His Only-Begotten Son, Jesus Christ

1. N. Gori, *Eucaristia. La mia autostrada per il Cielo. Biogrfia di Carlo Acutis*, 81. Cf. also 542.

2. 291.

3. Among the many possible examples, cf. Thomas Aquinas, *Summa Theologica*, First Part, q. 43.

4. Second Vatican Council, Constitution on the Liturgy, *Sacrosanctum Concilium*, December 4, 1963, 7.

Chapter 11: That Jesus Christ Be Loved and Known

1. Gori, *Eucaristia* …, 81. Cf. 542.

2. Gori, *Eucaristia* …, 81.

Chapter 12: A Life Truly Beautiful

1. 313.

2. For further information, allow me to refer to G. M. Carbone, *Ma la più grande di tutte è la carità*, 2nd ed., ESD, Bologna 2020.

Chapter 13: Dying to Ourselves Every Day

1. 291.

2. R. E. Brown, *The Anchor Bible, vol. 29: The Gospel According to John*, Doubleday, Garden City, New York, 1966, 475.

3. Cf. K. Wengst, *Il Vangelo di Giovanni*, Queriniana, Brescia, 2005, 495.

4. X. Leon-Dufour, *Lettura dell'Evangelo secondo Giovanni*, San Paolo, Cinisello Balsamo, 1992, vol. 2, 578.

5. R. Fabris, *Giovanni. Traduzione e commento*, Borla, Rome, 1992, 684. Brown, *The Gospel According to John*, 473: he demonstrates that the verb *apollynai* can be translated as *destroy*, making a stronger contrast with *preserve*.

6. Cf. A. Wikenhauser, *L'Evangelo secondo Giovanni tradotto e commentato*, Morcelliana, Brescia, 1962, 320.

7. Fabris, *Giovanni*, 685–686.

8. Wengst, *Il Vangelo di Giovanni*, 495.

9. R. Schnackenburg, *Il Vangelo di Giovanni*, Paideia, Brescia, 1973, II, 642.

10. Cf. G. M. Carbone, *Introduzione*, in L. Chardon, *La Croce di Gesù*, 2nd ed., ESD, Bologna 2018, 59–61.

Chapter 14: Climbing Golgotha

1. 313.

2. Cf. J. Ratzinger/Benedict XVI, *Gesù di Nazaret. Dall'ingresso in Gerusalemme fino alla risurrezione*, Libreria Editrice Vaticana, Vatican City, 2011, 165–187.

3. Rose of Lima, "Ad medicum Castillo," in *The Office of Readings According to the Roman Rite*, St. Paul Editions, Boston, 1983, 1528.

4. *Roman Missal,* Antiphon for the hymn *Pange, lingua*, Liturgy of Good Friday.

Chapter 15: Conquering Self

1. 291.

2. L. Scupoli, *The Spiritual Combat*, Rivingtons, London, 1875, 284–285.

3. J. Escrivá de Balaguer, *Camino*, Ares, Milan, 2012, No. 225.

4. *The Imitation of Christ*, I, 11, 6.

5. L. Chardon, *La Croce di Gesù*, 2nd ed., ESD, Bologna, 2018, No. 810.

Chapter 16: Frequenting the Sacraments

1. 292.

2. *Catechism of the Catholic Church*, 1127.

3. Vatican II, *Sacrosanctum Concilium*, 59, a passage reproduced in the *Catechism of the Catholic Church*, 1123.

4. *CCC* 1129.

5. Augustine, *Confessiones*, III, 11, 19, Bertelsmann, Gütersloh, 1876, 65.

Chapter 17: Being Pleasing to God

1. 294.

2. Thérèse of the Child Jesus, *Manuscrits autobiographiques*, Carmel de Lisieux, Lisieux, 1957, 313.

Chapter 18: The Highway to Heaven

1. 316.

2. M.-V. Bernadot, *De l'Eucharistie à la Trinité*, Bureaux du Rosaire, Marseilles, 1918, 30–31; which in turn cites Augustine, *Confessions*, vii, 10, 16.

3. J. R. R. Tolkien, *The Return of the King*, Houghton Mifflin, Boston, 1965, 213.

Chapter 19: Great Fortune

1. 316.

2. *CCC* 1085.

Chapter 20: Medicine of the Soul

1. 299.

2. 299. See Ignatius of Antioch, *Letter to the Ephesians*, in Hermigild Dressler, et. al. (eds.), *The Fathers of the Church: A New Translation*, Catholic University of America Press, Washington, D.C., 1947, 95.

3. 151, Nos. 94 and 97.

4. 278.

5. J. R. R. Tolkien, *Letter 250*, in id., *The Letters of J. R. R. Tolkien*, Houghton Mifflin, Boston, 1981, 338–339.

Chapter 21: Jesus, Go Ahead and Get Comfortable

1. 297.

2. 317.

Chapter 22: Always United with Jesus

1. 293.

2. This is the translation proposed by X. Leon-Dufour, *Lettura dell'Evangelo secondo Giovanni*, San Paolo, Cinisello Balsamo, 1995, vol. 3, 373 and 387. I also follow his translation for v. 22.

3. R. Schnackenburg, *Il Vangelo di Giovanni*, Parte terza, Paideia, Brescia, 1981, 304–305.

4. Cf. Léon-Dufour, *Lettura dell'Evangelo secondo Giovanni*, vol. 3, 388.

Chapter 23: My Guardian Angels

1. 297.

2. Bernard of Clairvaux, sermon on the Song of Songs, in *The Liturgy of the Hours*, Catholic Book Pub. Co., New York, 1975, 125.

Chapter 24: I'm Coming to Mass, Too

1. 147.

2. Cf. 185. Debora Zauli, Antonia Salzano's cousin, also recalls that "he went to Mass every day without being made to go, and went very naturally," 223.

3. 253; cf. also 254.

4. 272.
5. 268.
6. 147.
7. 223.

Chapter 25: Whole Persons, Made in His Image

1. 171.

Chapter 26: The Eucharist Is the Heart of Christ

1. 171.
2. cf. Ratzinger/Benedict XVI, *Gesù di Nazaret*, 148–149.
3. Published by Edizioni Studio Domenicano, Bologna, 1997. Here I quote from p. 101.

Chapter 27: We Will Increase Our Capacity to Love

1. 291.
2. Léon-Dufour, *Lettura dell'Evangelo secondo Giovanni*, vol. 2, 218.
3. *Roman Missal*, Eucharistic Prayer III. Similar words are also found in Eucharistic Prayer II: "Humbly we pray that, partaking of the Body and Blood of Christ, we may be gathered into one by the Holy Spirit."

Chapter 28: We Are Beloved Disciples

1. 314.
2. R. Schnackenburg, *Il Vangelo di Giovanni*, Parte terza, Paideia, Brescia, 1981, 623–644; here I cite 641–642.
3. Léon-Dufour, *Lettura dell'Evangelo secondo Giovanni*, vol. 3, 58.
4. Ibid., note 66.
5. Ibid.
6. cf. 314.

Chapter 29: Give Us This Day the Daily Eucharist, Too

1. 317 and 523.
2. Origen, *La preghiera*, 27, 1-2, Città Nuova, Rome, 1997, 130–131.
3. Cyprian, *The Our Father*, 18, CCSL 3A, 101–102.
4. Jerome, *Commento a Matteo*, I, 6, 11, Città Nuova, Romem 1969, 51.

Chapter 30: The Lord Is There

1. 167. Cf. 337; 340.

2. 353 and 532. It is the testimony of Antonia Salzano that allows us to date this episode, 321.

Chapter 31: Jerusalem Is Right at Our Doorstep

1. 168.

2. 316.

3. 316. Cf. 317 and 524.

Chapter 32: True Beauty

1. Antonia Salzano, Andrea Acutis, *Trasmettere la fede alla scuola di nostro figlio Carlo*, ESD, Bologna, 2023, 137.

Chapter 33: Lines and Lines

1. 316, cf. 524.

2. R. Coggi, *Dialogo sull'Eucaristia. Incontrare, conoscere, amare Gesù "pane della vita,"* ESD, Bologna, 1997, 26–27.

3. No. 1374.

Chapter 34: Unbloody Sacrifice

1. 314.

2. Ratzinger/Benedict XVI, *Gesù di Nazaret*, 104.

3. No. 1365.

4. Bernadot, *De l'Eucharistie à la Trinité*, 136.

Chapter 35: The Consecration

1. 316.

2. *CCC* 1377.

3. *CCC* 1369.

Chapter 36: Jesus Is Very Original

1. 316.

2. Chardon, *La croce di Gesù*, No. 340.

3. Ibid., No. 528.

Chapter 37: The Victory

1. 315.

2. Cf. 315.

Chapter 38: To Thank Jesus

1. 524.

2. Bernadot, *De l'Eucharistie à la Trinité*, 132.

Chapter 39: The Miracle of the Donkey of Rimini

1. 541. Cf. Gori, *L'Eucaristia ...*, 75.

2. Cf. Istituto San Clemente, S. Meloni, *I miracoli eucaristici e le radici cristiane dell'Europa*, expanded and updated 3rd edition, ESD, Bologna, 2014, 38–40.

Chapter 40: The Sacred Heart of Jesus Is the Eucharist

1. 317. Cf. also 525 and 171: "The Eucharist is the heart of Christ," as Rajesh Mohur reports.

2. F. Serafini, *Un cardiologo visita Gesù. I miracoli eucaristici alla prova della scienza*, revised and corrected 2nd edition, ESD, Bologna, 2019.

3. *Roman Missal*, third typical edition, 2011.

Chapter 41: He Who Criticizes the Church Criticizes Himself

1. 312.

2. Cf. also chapter 22.

3. G. Biffi, *Homily*, given in Bologna on June 2, 1985.

Chapter 42: Confessing Sins

1. 229.

2. 254.

Chapter 43: The Hot-Air Balloon

1. 530.

2. 321.

Chapter 44: Conversion

1. Salzano, Acutis, *Trasmettere la fede*, 48.

Chapter 45: If We Knew What Eternity Is

1. Salzano, Acutis, *Trasmettere la fede*, 50–51.

Chapter 46: Loving Others

1. Salzano, Acutis, *Trasmettere la fede*, 30.

Chapter 47: Grave Sins

1. 322.

2. The Hebrew verb *nāfal* and the Greek *piptō* have roughly the same breadth of meaning, and mean to fall, to plunge, to collapse, and, therefore, in a translated sense, to sin: cf. W. Bauder, Πίπτω, in L. Coenen, E. Beyreuther, H. Bietenhard, *Dizionario dei concetti biblici del Nuovo Testamento*, EDB, Bologna, 1991, 185–188. The Hebrew noun *kat'at*, which means 'lack,' *'āwōn*, which means 'guilt' as a deliberate deviation from the right path, and *pesh'a*, which means 'rebellion,' constitute a group of concepts that is rendered with the Greek noun *hamartía*, which literally means a lack, a failure to reach a goal. *Hamartía* and the verb *hamartanō* come from the root *hamart-*, which means to miss, to fail; it indicates all that goes against the right and the just — that is, the *orthón*. Finally, the Greek, to signify the action of sinning, also uses *parabaínō*, which literally means "I go astray, I fail, I deviate." In the Old Testament it is used in the translated sense of deviating from the covenant, abandoning God.

3. I venture to refer to G. M. Carbone, *Morale della legge. La legge senza timore*, ESD, Bologna, 2020, 235 Günter 281, where I dwell on the value of the "new commandment" and its relationship with the person of Jesus Christ and the Holy Spirit.

Chapter 48: The Outstretched Hands of Christ

1. 372.

2. Vatican II, Dogmatic Constitution on the Church, *Lumen Gentium*, No. 10.

3. Coggi, *Piccolo Catechismo Eucaristico*, 4th ed., 30.

Chapter 49: Jesus and the Pope

1. 353.

Chapter 50: The Heart of Jesus and the Heart of Mary

1. 171.
2. Cf. 318 and 371.
3. *Roman Missal*, third typical edition.

Chapter 51: Always Close to My Heart

1. 296.

Chapter 52: If God Possesses Our Heart

1. Salzano, Acutis, *Trasmettere la fede*, 40–41.

Chapter 53: Infinity Our Goal

1. Salzano, Acutis, *Trasmettere la fede*, 47.
2. See below, chapter 100, the poem dedicated to distraction.

Chapter 54: The Only Woman in My Life

1. 316.
2. Cf. 154.
3. Cf. 319.
4. Cf. 192.

Chapter 55: He Listens

1. Salzano, Acutis, *Trasmettere la fede*, 27.

Chapter 56: I Come to Tell Jesus about Things

1. 117.

Chapter 57: If You Open Your Heart to God

1. 172.

Chapter 58: The Lord Will Let Me Know

1. 119.
2. *The Imitation of Christ*, II, 4, 1.

Chapter 59: Pray Very Much for Sinners

1. 264.
2. 271.

Chapter 60: Our Prayers

1. 298.
2. Thomas Aquinas, *Summa Theologica*, Third Part, q. 89, a. 5.

Chapter 61: He Is in Purgatory

1. 185.
2. 295.
3. 373.
4. 271.
5. Cf. 316.

Chapter 62: I Saw Jesus

1. 373.
2. Chardon, *La Croce di Gesù*, No. 972.
3. Augustine, *Sermon*, 34, 5, NBA XXIX, 1, 626–627.

Chapter 63: The Rosary

1. 151.
2. 152.

Chapter 64: Is It All the Same?

1. 302.

Chapter 65: It Doesn't Weigh on Me

1. 202; cf. 206.
2. 362. Cf. also the testimony of another classmate, Tommaso, 207.

Chapter 66: I'll Gladly Come Give You a Hand

1. 206.
2. 203.

Chapter 67: I Wasn't Hungry Today Anyway

1. 203.

Chapter 68: Reaching Out to Someone Who Has Made a Mistake

1. 174.

Chapter 69: He's Much Better Than Me

1. 153.

2. *The Imitation of Christ*, I, 7, 3.

Chapter 70: Humility

1. Salzano, Acutis, *Trasmettere la fede*, 55–56.

Chapter 71: The Light of Others

1. Salzano, Acutis, *Trasmettere la fede*, 139–140.

Chapter 72: Sadness and Happiness

1. 303, 324.

2. Catherine of Siena, *Le lettere di S. Caterina da Siena*, vol. 1, Barbèra, Florence, 1860, 136–137.

Chapter 73: You Can't Take It with You

1. 268.

2. 173.

Chapter 74: I'm Interested

1. 144; cf. 140.

2. 170. His friend Jacopo from Assisi also testifies: "He knew the *Catechism of the Catholic Church* really well, and I sometimes practiced the answers to the Catechism with him. He was a big help," 256.

3. 166.

4. Cf. 271.

Chapter 75: Get Him to Be Less Fanatical

1. 166.

2. Cf. G. Amorth, *Dietro un sorriso. Alessandrina Maria da Costa*, Paoline, Cinisello Balsamo, 1992.

Chapter 76: Like All Houses

1. Cf. 305 and 438.

2. Cf. Thomas Aquinas, *Summa Theologica*, II-II, q. 167, a. 1 co.

3. Augustine, *Of the Morals of the Catholic Church*, in M. Dods (ed.), *The Works of Aurelius Augustine, Bishop of Hippo*, vol. 5, T & T

Clark, Edinburgh, 1872, 26.

4. *The Imitation of Christ*, I, 2, 2; and I, 11, 1.

Chapter 77: Nobles

1. 306.

2. Cf. J.-P. Torrell, *Amico della verità. Vita e opere di Tommaso d'Aquino*, 3rd ed., ESD, Bologna, 2017, 28–32.

3. Thomas Aquinas, *De rationibus fidei*, ed. Leonina, t. XL, Rome, 1969, 56.

Chapter 78: I'll Take It to My Parents

1. 242.

Chapter 79: I'll Get My Dad, He'll Understand

1. 378.

2. 287.

Chapter 80: Blind and Deluded

1. 541. Cf. Gori, *L'Eucaristia …*, 70.

2. *The Imitation of Christ*, II, 5, 1.

3. Ibid., III, 46, 1-2.

4. For more, see Carbone, *Ma la più grande di tutte è la carità*, 295–299.

Chapter 81: Being True Always Pays Off

1. 241.

2. 126.

3. These traits are recalled by his classmates and teachers, cf. deposition of Michele, 131.

4. 371.

Chapter 82: Holy Temple or Fire-Eater's Puppets?

1. 231.

2. 311.

3. 137.

4. 390.

5. 311.

6. 312.

Chapter 83: It's Still Too Soon

1. 204.

2. 169.

Chapter 84: My True Love Is for Jesus

1. 175.

2. Catherine of Siena, *Letter 21*, to a recipient whose name is withheld, *Le Lettere*, vol. 3, ESD, Bologna, 1999, 498.

Chapter 85: Killing of an Innocent

1. 390. Cf. also the testimonies of Silvia, 126; of his eighth-grade classmates, Giovanni M., 189, and Tommaso V., 207; of Alberto T., a high school classmate, 200.

2. 392.

3. 133.

4. 163.

5. 133; cf. also the testimonies of his eighth-grade classmates, Giovanni M., 189, and Tommaso V., 207.

Chapter 86: Computer Scientist

1. 302.

2. 176.

3. *Un genio dell'informatica in cielo. Biografia del servo di Dio Carlo Acutis*. Published by Libreria Editrice Vaticana, Vatican City, 2016. An English translation of this work is *Carlo Acutis: The First Millennial Saint*, published by Our Sunday Visitor, Huntington, Indiana, 2021.

Chapter 87: Assisi

1. 371. His parents also confirm that "he felt very happy in Assisi," 326.

Chapter 88: Fátima

1. 537.

Chapter 89: Hell

1. 318 and 529.
2. *The Imitation of Christ*, I, 21, 5.

Chapter 90: I've Put on Seventy Kilos …

1. 323.
2. Cf. 273–274.
3. 323.
4. 269.
5. *The Imitation of Christ*, I, 24, 7.
6. 173.

Chapter 91: The Lord Has Given Me a Wake-Up Call

1. 270, 284, 324.
2. 270; cf. 284; 325.
3. 223.
4. Barzaghi, *Lo sguardo della sofferenza*, 95.

Chapter 92: There Are People Who Suffer more Than Me

1. 278 and 324.
2. 289.
3. Cf. 326–327.

Chapter 93: I'm Heading for Peace

1. 173.

Chapter 94: Passing on to Co-Eternity

1. Salzano, Acutis, *Trasmettere la fede*, 34.

Chapter 95: Alexander Sauli

1. Cf. statement of Luana Pennino, maternal grandmother, 279; testimony of Andrea Acutis, 290.
2. Biffi, *Homily …*, June 13, 2008.

Chapter 96: I Offer to the Lord

1. 167.
2. Cf. testimony of Antonia Salzano, 283.

3. 269; cf. 278.

4. 323.

5. On the difference in usage between *didōmi* ("I give," "I offer") and *títhēmi* ("I present," "I deliver"), cf. Léon-Dufour, *Lettura dell'Evangelo secondo Giovanni*, vol. 2, 461–466.

6. Cf. Thomas Aquinas, *Summa Theologica*, First Part, q. 37 for "Love"; q. 38 for "Gift."

7. On the oblative aspect of charity, cf. Carbone, *Ma la più grande di tutte è la carità*, 86–88; 113–114; 124; 376.

8. Common of the Blessed Virgin Mary (Prayer over the Offerings, option 2), *Roman Missal*, third typical edition, 2011.

9. Ibid., 434.

Chapter 97: Lamb

1. Cf. Gori, *Eucaristia …*, 28.

2. 297.

3. 290.

Chapter 98: Kit for Becoming Saints

1. Salzano, Acutis, *Trasmettere la fede*, 154-155.

You might also like:

Carlo Acutis
The First Millennial Saint

By Nicola Gori

This biography, written by the postulator of Carlo Acutis' cause for canonization, demonstrates the ways he was a little "different" at school, in the pizzerias, and on the soccer field. What set Carlo apart was his constant pursuit of holiness. Carlo loved to attend daily Mass and frequent Eucharistic adoration. The Word of God and the Eucharist were the center of his life. Carlo's unwavering devotion to the Eucharist inspired him to tell the story of Eucharistic miracles through a website he created just for fun.

You might also like:

My Son Carlo: Carlo Acutis Through the Eyes of His Mother

By Antonia Salzano Acutis with Paolo Rodari

Even with the worldwide attention on this millennial saint, we're left wondering and wanting more. What was Carlo really like? How did he interact with those closest to him in daily life? What was it like to live in the same home as him?

Antonia Salzano Acutis shares for the first time the intimate, private moments of her son's life, including his final days in vivid detail before he died from leukemia at the age of 15. In her own words, Antonia shares stories and memories as a mother who lost her son too early but was forever shaped by his remarkable life.